BITING the MORAL BULLET

ISSUES OF PEACE AND JUSTICE

**Edited by
Kevin O'Donnell**

**Foreword by
Bruce Kent**

Hodder & Stoughton

A MEMBER OF THE HODDER HEADLINE GROUP

Acknowledgements

Contributors

Marigold Bentley, Religious Society of Friends
Pippa Bobbett, Oxford Development Education Centre (ODEC)
Pat Gaffney, Pax Christi
Bruce Kent
Stephanie Koorey, Campaign Against Arms Trade (CAAT)
Jan Melichar, Peace Pledge Union
Kevin O'Donnell
Lib Peck, National Peace Council
Helena Stride, Imperial War Museum
Simon Wilkinson

Illustrations by Peter Hudspith

The publishers would like to thank the following for permission to reproduce copyright material in this volume:

Central Office of Information for extracts from *Your life in the Royal Navy* and *The World at your feet: Women in the RAF*; Faber & Faber for an extract from *GOTCHA!: Media, the Government and the Falkland Crisis*, Robert Harris; the *Financial Times* for 'Fighting on foreign soil', Victoria Griffith; *The Guardian* for 'Arms Trade – Deadly Global Arms Jamboree'; Leslie and Arthur Harrison for an extract from William Harrison's presentation to the Military Tribunal (1916); HarperCollins Publishers Ltd for extracts from *Building the Global Village*, Bruce Kent and *Towers of Trebizond*, Rose Macaulay; *The Observer* for 'East Timor: Secret Killing of a Nation', Hugh O'Shaughnessy; *The Times* for an extract from 'We are all Falklanders now' © Times Newspapers Ltd, 1982.

Every effort has been made to trace and acknowledge ownership of copyright. The publishers will be glad to make suitable arrangements with any copyright holders whom it has not been possible to contact.

British Library Cataloguing in Publication Data

Biting the moral bullet: issues of peace and justice
  1. Conflict management 2. Mediation, International
  I. O'Donnell, Kevin, 1957–
  327.1'72

ISBN 0 340 66410X

First published 1997
Impression number   10 9 8 7 6 5 4 3 2 1
Year   1999 1998 1997

Typeset by Wearset, Boldon, Tyne and Wear.
Printed in Great Britain for Hodder & Stoughton Educational, a division of Hodder Headline Plc, 338 Euston Road, London NW1 3BH by Hobbs the Printers, Totton, Hampshire.

Contents

Foreword

The original idea for this book came to me as the result of a series of visits to secondary schools which I made in 1993 and 1994.

The aim of those visits was to try to help young people to understand that war and the preparations for war are amongst the greatest causes of world poverty and environmental damage. There is an intimate inter-connection.

I soon realised that I was so often on a very different wavelength to those year 11 and year 12/13 students I was meeting. Many of them felt that, however weighty were the problems of the world, there was nothing they could do about them anyway.

So I spent much time talking about courageous individuals and groups who have, over the years, made positive change possible. Moreover, there were all sorts of assumptions about war, injustice, and conflict that I found I had to challenge. Time and again I would be told that war is inevitable: it is in the nature of human beings to fight. Alongside such assumptions often ran a near total ignorance of such international peacemaking institutions, especially the United Nations and its agencies, as do exist.

So I came to believe that a down-to-earth resourcebook would be a help to pupils and teachers. It is however easy to have ideas. Without the co-operation of those who know much more about the world of education than I do, the idea would have remained just an idea.

As it is, this useful book has now seen the light of day.

Bruce Kent

Introduction

'Peace and Justice' provides the teacher with schemes of work and Activity Sheets for aspects of KS4 RE or PSE, or year 12/13 General Studies. Some of the material is interactive, using role play, discussion and group work. Some materials are more information based, to use as a general resource. Individual units can be used independently of each other if so desired. This book should make a contribution to Citizenship education.

The book has been produced by a team of people, some from an educational background, some from committed work in the area of justice and peace campaigning. Contributions have come from different stances. There is a concern to promote peace education but with a good and healthy balance, allowing different points of view to be heard. There is also a concern to root peace education within everyday pupil experience – tips for solving small and ordinary conflicts can be used for more global issues, up to a point.

The inspiration for this book came from my visit to a Peace Education day at Friend's House in Euston, where there were many lively contributions and ideas, as well as numerous small press materials. This all needed sifting through, but there was an obvious need to flag this up in an accessible format for as many teachers as possible. The second point of inspiration was a visit by Bruce Kent to my school. Here was a seasoned peace campaigner full of energy and ideas. I just had to tap some of his experience and distill it in an accessible package.

Thanks must go to the Imperial War museum for their support. Wads of material were provided. A full account of their educational services may be found in the Appendix. A special thanks is also due to the Peace Pledge Union who have allowed us to adapt and use material from their *Peace and War* book.

Kevin O'Donnell (Editor)

Student Introduction

The two pictures above show scenes from protests at Greenham Common Airbase, near Newbury, in the 1980s. Greenham Common was a US airbase where nuclear missiles were kept in case of war. A peace camp grew up around the base, which became exclusively for women. They protested by chanting, handing out leaflets, blocking access to the base, and by performing symbolic actions. They linked arms around the base, forming a circle of life. Their womanhood, and motherhood, symbolised life attempting to overcome a force of death and disaster. Another symbolic act was to hang children's toys from the fence, to highlight the horror of what was being planned in the base – the potential destruction of ordinary human beings. Gradually, with the collapse of communism and different relationships with the East, many of the US bases were closed in the UK or emptied of nuclear weapons. How much good had the women done? They felt they had made a stand, and raised awareness among the public. They saw the presence of nuclear weapons on our soil as an obscenity and a threat to peace.

The people running the base would have had a very different idea. They were trying to keep the peace. Horrific though nuclear weapons were, they thought that having them would scare people into not using them on us. Thus there was a balance of power, a stalemate which would prevent a major war breaking out. The soldiers thought they were doing their duty for democracy, to help preserve our way of life.

Who would you agree with more, the women or the soldiers? Why?

People have different ideas about what helps peace and what creates justice. They have deep and strong convictions. We will explore some of these and help you to form your own opinions.

A The Individual

① Dealing With Your Own Anger

Lesson One

AIM

To encourage students to think about themselves in relation to what makes them angry and what might cause them to be violent.

OBJECTIVES

Through the course of the lesson the student should be able to name/pinpoint aspects of their lives which they need to recognise as making them angry. Through thinking and discussing this topic, it may help them to be able to deal with difficulties without resorting to violence.

RESOURCES

Activity sheet 1.

METHOD (40 minute lesson)

1 Introduction of topic by teacher (using opening paragraph if necessary).

2 Division of class into small groups – not more than 5 persons in each group. Make instructions about exercise clear and distribute sheets.

3 Let groups discuss and make their choices.

4 Feedback from each group in turn with their choices and why.

Possible follow-on work

Seville Statement on violence (see Appendix 2) – materials available from CEWC.

Project work on looking for accounts of violence in newspapers or descriptions of violence on TV news.

Discussion work on what makes a peaceful society e.g. police force, courts, health care, shelter etc.

Discussion work on ways of using energy when you feel angry.

Feelings exercises should only be done with groups who are fairly familiar with one another. The feelings work on Activity Sheet 1 can be given to students to take home and think about. It does not necessarily need to be a classroom lesson. Use this for discussion only if you are sure that the feelings the students reveal to one another will not be used by them to hurt each other on other occasions.

ACTIVITY SHEET
Understanding Our Own Anger and Violence

We all get angry about things that happen to us. We all have the ability to hurt other people both verbally and physically. Some of us carry anger with us all of the time and it may take only a little incident to spark off a row. Others go through life as if nothing ever touched them. We have all had different experiences in life and have memories which inform us about the present. In order to come to terms with the fact that all of us have the capacity to be angry and violent, it is important to explore our own feelings about the causes of them.

Ranking Exercise – Violence Is Caused By . . .

> In groups read and discuss the following statements and order them according to which you agree and disagree with. Rank them in order 1 to 6. 1 would be the statement the group agrees with most and 6 agrees with least.

There will never be peace in the world because it is human nature to be violent.

Humans are peaceful – they learn how to be violent.

In groups and crowds, all humans become violent.

If people do not have means to channel their aggression, they become violent.

People are violent because there is too much violence on television and in films.

People must be punished if they are violent, then there will be more peace.

Feelings Exercise – I Get Angry When . . .

This exercise is really for yourself so that you can think about what makes you angry and unhappy. You might then like to look at how to deal with these when you come across them in your daily lives.

I get angry when . . .

I get impatient when . . .

I am happy when . . .

. . . frighten me.

I get on well with these sorts of people . . .

② Exploring Everyday Conflicts

Lesson One

AIM

To encourage students to look creatively at conflicts in their lives and how they can deal with them.

OBJECTIVES

To teach strategies to deal with conflicts including problem solving techniques, listening skills and an introduction to the process of mediation.

RESOURCES

Activity Sheets 2, 3.

METHOD

Inflammatory language

1 As a whole class, ask the students what words they like to hear said about them and to them. List these on a board or flipchart.

2 Ask them what words they do not like to hear said about them or to them. List them. Distribute Activity Sheet 2. In groups of 5, focus on the words they do not like to hear. Ask the groups for a list of reasons why those words might be used.

3 Then list what the students *do* when they have things they do not like said to them.

This exercise can give 'ammunition' to those students who deliberately want to hurt each other. Thus it needs to be undertaken in a spirit of trust with the teacher emphasising the negative results of verbal abuse.

Identifying the problem

1 Distribute Activity Sheet 3 with the statements to small groups of students and ask them to identify what the central problem is and what they would do about it.

2 Collect feedback from each group and discuss any differences.

Lesson Two

RESOURCES

Information Sheets 4, 5, 6; Activity Sheet 7.

INTRODUCING MEDIATION

Mediation is a form of problem solving. An uninvolved and unbiased person is invited to listen to two sides of a dispute. They help the two people, or groups, through a process where a settlement is agreed. **Arbitration** is totally different. Here, a third party decides an outcome.

METHOD

1 Divide the class into groups of 3. If there are extra people they can be used as observers.

2 Distribute the role sheets, with a Big Grey, Little Red and a mediator in each group. Explain what has to be done – read through the role and allow the mediator to explain the process they are a part of. (Mediators might need some help.)

3 Give them at least 15 minutes to thoroughly explore possible solutions.

4 Bring them back together in the whole group and ask the following questions: What solutions did you come to? How did it feel to be a mediator/grey/red? What similarities do you see between this and real life situations? How useful do you think the role of the mediator is? Where else do you think mediation could be used?

MEDIATING YOUR OWN PROBLEMS

METHOD

In small groups, ask the students to create their own 'real life' problem between two people. Suggest that they start with the typical types of arguments they have with their friends. Role play the problem with one person taking each side and one or two people mediating with them using the instructions for mediation from the former role play. Activity Sheet 7 might be particularly helpful here. Use this to talk about the practical application of mediation. Could it be used in your school?

2 **ACTIVITY SHEET**
Inflammatory Language

The words we say to each other can hurt or help. They can make us feel sad or happy. In groups, discuss the things that you like to hear about yourself, and the things that you do not like to hear. List five examples for each, below.

Words You Want to Hear About Yourself

1 _____
2 _____
3 _____
4 _____
5 _____

Words That You Do Not Want to Hear About Yourself

1 _____
2 _____
3 _____
4 _____
5 _____

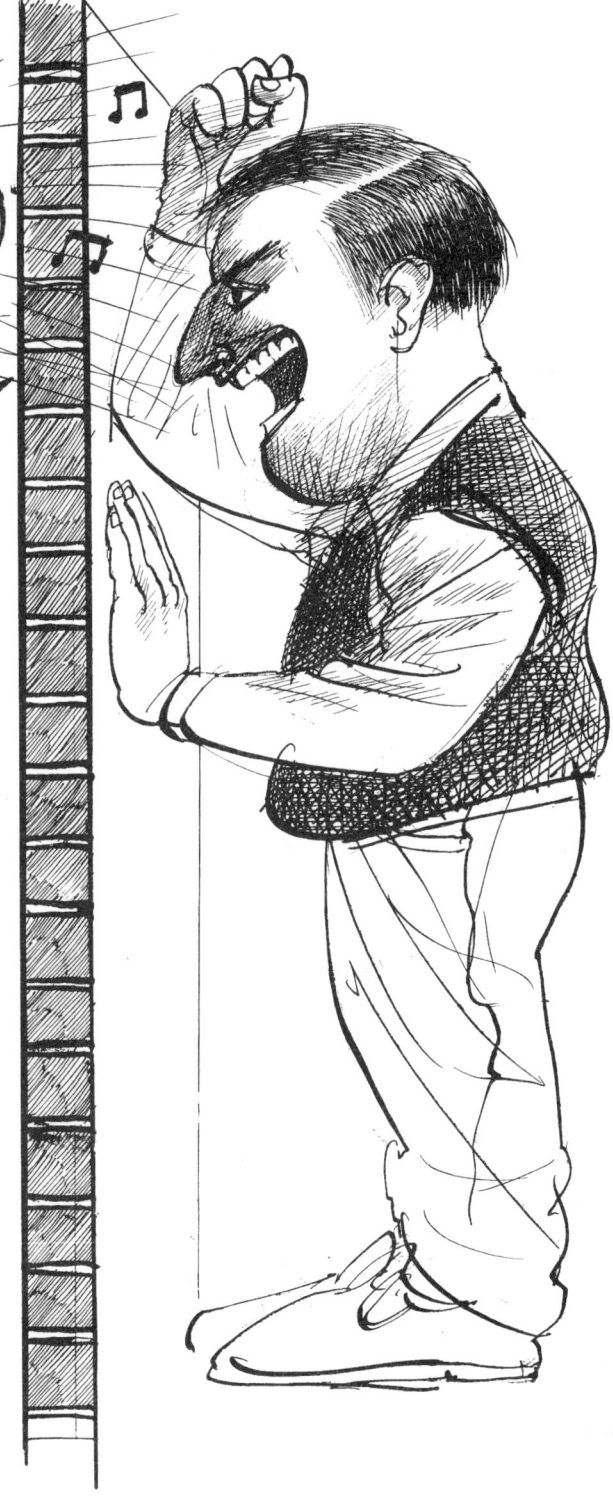

- 'It's all his fault. Whenever I play my music he bangs on the wall then Mum complains and I get into trouble. If he didn't bang on the wall it would be OK.'

- 'She used to be my best friend but I can't trust her with my boyfriend. She is always hanging round him pretending to talk to me. She flirts all the time.'

- 'I don't mind lending my clothes usually but last time she took that skirt, it came back with a coffee stain on the front. She didn't even apologise.'

- 'She can't stop swearing. She came round to my house and my Mum opened the door – I was really embarrassed when she started talking in her usual way.'

- 'Me and my mates always mess around and have a good laugh but last week on the way home things went a bit wrong. Instead of just teasing this little kid from around the corner, we started to rough him up – and hit him and kick him too. We were stopped by a neighbour and we ran away.'

Identify the central problem in these situations. What would you do about it?

You are Big Grey. Your ancestors have lived in the forest for many generations. The forest used to be much bigger and your ancestors used to roam freely and find plenty of food in the forest. There was a small village at the edge of the forest, but the settlers who lived there did not trouble your tribe and you had very little to do with them.

It is very different now. The village grew and grew into a large town and much of the forest has been cut down. The settlers have been hunting the Big Greys and there are not many of you left. There is also very little food left to find in what remains of the forest, so you are forced to look for food at the edges of the town and steal from the settlers. Life has become very dangerous.

Yesterday, you met a young settler called Little Red. She was carrying some delicious food in a basket, going along the path the settlers built through what was once part of the forest, but is now one of

their 'parks'. You asked her for some food, but she refused rudely. You gathered that she was visiting her grandmother in the old part of the town. So you ran ahead, quickly shut the old woman in the cupboard and took her place in the bed, hurriedly putting on some of her clothes. When Little Red arrived, you tried to get the food from her, but she must have recognised you because she screamed and made an awful fuss so that a whole load of settlers armed with nasty weapons came after you and you were lucky to escape – still starving.

Luckily, it seems as if there is some kind of Mediation Service which has been set up in the town to help sort out arguments. You think that this might give you a chance to put your side of the story and they have invited you to come along with a guarantee of safe passage, so you go along to meet the Mediator and Little Red.

You live with your mother in the town which has been built near the edge of the forest. Your mother has to work very hard to get enough money to feed you both and to pay for the other necessities. Your grandmother lives in the old part of the town, which was originally just a small village. She is a very independent old lady and wants to live in the small cottage where she lived all her life. But she is getting frail and cannot really feed herself each day, so you take her one meal a day, which your mother has prepared. The only way to her house (other than going a very long way round) takes you through the park which was once part of the forest. You have heard that Big Greys still live in the forest and sometimes wander into the park. You are rather frightened, but dare not tell your mother as she has enough troubles already.

Yesterday, as you were going to grandmother's house, a Big Grey suddenly came up to you and asked for food. Naturally, you tried to get rid of him, but you must have said something about where you were going. When you got to grandmother's house, you noticed that she was in bed and looked very strange. She asked you odd questions and was very eager to grab the food. As she reached towards you, you suddenly recognised Big Grey. Of course you screamed for help and were very relieved when some builders and gardeners who worked next door, rushed in with their tools and chased the Big Grey away. You have been invited to talk to Big Grey in the presence of the new Mediation Service which tries to sort out problems in the town. You have heard Big Greys are dying out as they do not have enough food in the forest, but you are mainly interested in knowing that you can safely deliver food for grandmother without frightening experiences like yesterday's.

The story you have heard:

Yesterday there was an incident when a Big Grey slunk up to a young girl named Little Red who was walking through the park to take food to her elderly grandmother who lives on her own. He asked for food, she was frightened and ran away. On entering her grandmother's house, she started talking to the figure in the bedroom whom she assumed to be her grandmother, only to find that it was Big Grey who (as it turned out) had shut the old lady in the cupboard and was now trying to trick Little Red into giving him the food. She shrieked for help and some neighbours, armed with garden tools, chased the Big Grey away. Both Big Grey and Little Red have agreed to come to the town Mediation Service.

(Note – you live in the town.)

Instruction for Mediation

1 First you explain to both of them that you are not part of the legal system and that you are there to help them towards an agreement. State that it is not your job to say who is right or wrong.

2 Try to make them feel comfortable and safe by agreeing ground rules with them about not interrupting, not shouting and point out that they need to listen to one another. State that the emphasis must be on co-operation.

3 Ask them to tell their side of the story one after the other. It is your job to listen to their stories.

4 Ask them what they think the essential problem is. Try to get them to agree on this.

5 Ask each of them how they feel about the situation.

6 Ask them what their ideal solution would be.

7 Using their ideal solution try to work on something which both could accept – this may not be a grand scheme but a step towards better relations.

8 Thank each party for their contribution.

7 ACTIVITY SHEET
Exploring Everyday Conflicts

Each of these scenes involves an argument. What is the problem? How might it be solved?

Role play these situations, and any others that you can think of. One person should play the part of a mediator.

B Society

❶ Gender Issues

Lesson One

AIM

To explore behaviour and gender roles.

RESOURCES

Activity Sheet 8.

METHOD

1 Start a general discussion on the types of behaviour – so you can draw up a list.

2 Get into mixed groups of five. Write down a list of things which make you similar. What are the differences between you?

3 Each group to share the information with the rest of the class.

4 Go back into the same small groups. Are you expected to behave in a certain way? Who expects you to behave in this way? Are there any differences between the way boys and girls are meant to behave?

5 Work through Activity Sheet 8.

8 ACTIVITY SHEET
Gender roles

Look at the pictures of girls and boys.
What do they say about girls and boys?
Do you agree with them?

② Civil Disobedience and Non-violence

AIM

To explore the meaning and practice of non-violence through contemporary examples.

OBJECTIVE

To have the students categorise some contemporary actions for peace and justice and then use these to encourage the students to produce some characteristics of non-violence in action.

Lesson One

RESOURCES

Information Sheets 9, 10; Activity Sheet 11.

METHOD

1 Introduce the theme, which is to look at a range of peace actions that have taken place during the 1980s and 90s.

2 As a whole class, ask the students to think of any peaceful action or event they have read or heard, about an issue of peace, third world concern, care for the environment. List these for all to see.

3 Give out Information Sheets 9, 10 and allow the students time to read through them. Do any of these actions match with what they have listed? Ask the students to work in groups of four on Activity Sheet 11 to categorise the events they have listed and those on the sheet.

4 Bring the groups together to discuss their responses to the last question on the Activity Sheet.

Lesson Two

RESOURCES

Activity Sheet 12.

METHOD

1 Recall the last session and variety of actions that can be undertaken for peace and justice. Some of these actions may have brought those involved into confrontation with laws of the state – not paying taxes, refusing to obey laws, occupying land etc.

Give the class this definition of non-violent civil disobedience:

'Non-violent actions that challenge something which is unjust or evil by non-cooperation with the state.' For many, this may mean refusing to obey unjust laws or breaking the law to expose something which is unjust or violent.

2 Give out Activity Sheet 12. Ask the students to work on their own to complete the form. When each student has finished ask them to work in groups of four to share their results.

3 With the whole class discuss which of the activities gained the most support and which the least.

Use these questions to develop the discussion on civil disobedience.

a) All of these actions involve some kind of risk to the people involved. What questions come to mind about making decisions to take part in such actions?

b) Are there times when the

traditional means of bringing about change e.g. voting, writing letters etc. are inadequate? Can you think of examples in this country or in other countries, when people have decided to take part in non-violent civil disobedience?

c) How important is it that civil disobedience is peaceful?

Lesson Three

RESOURCES

Activity Sheet 13.

METHOD

1 Introduce the topic, which is an extension of work that has been done looking at contemporary models of peace action in the 80s–90s. The last session ended by raising a question about the 'peaceful' nature of actions.

2 Invite the students to brainstorm on what they understand by the word 'non-violence'. Keep a record of the responses.

3 Divide into groups of four. Give out Activity Sheet 13 and ask the students to read through these and then work through the discussion points at the end. Ask each group to come up with a definition of non-violence based on their discussion. Share these with the whole class.

4 Points for general discussion.

a) Is non-violent action something that anyone can do or does it have to be planned and prepared for?

b) From the definitions that have been given, is non-violence simply a strategy, a way of doing things, or could it change the way we actually live and organise ourselves in society?

c) Can you think of any ways in which your school could provide training in non-violence to help students take more responsibility for their own lives?

INFORMATION SHEET
Non-violent Actions in the 1980s and 90s

1980s Thousands of Americans **sign pledges** to take part in non-violent protests if the US military invade Nicaragua.

A group called 'witness for peace' sends thousands of Americans to Nicaragua to form a **'shield of love'** to help stop U.S. military violence.

1981–89 Thousands of women take part in non-violent activities at **Greenham Common** in Berkshire to protest against the siting of American cruise nuclear missiles in England. Over the years many are arrested, taken to court and imprisoned for, among other things, entering the base and exposing missile silos, stopping the cruise missile convoy leaving the base.

1986 In the Philippines ordinary people **take to the streets to stop the military** and in non-violent actions help bring down the dictatorship of President Marcos. This was known as 'people power'.

1988 In South Africa during the apartheid regime, 143 white's **refuse to do military service** with the South African Defence Force.

1991 In Belgrade, a group called 'Women in Black' **appeared weekly on the streets to protest against the war in Croatia**. Over the months they were joined by other women and continued their protest although they are often exposed to insults by those who pass by.

1994 Protestors **occupy houses and trees** in East London to prevent contractors from bulldozing houses and vegetation to make way for a new road system. This is one of many such actions that have taken place in Britain over the past two years.

1994 Thousands of people in London take part in actions **(sitting on the roof of parliament, holding a mass rally in Hyde Park)** to protest against the Criminal Justice Bill.

The Peasants of Larzac Say No

Larzac is a limestone plateau in southern France famous for its cheese. A small military camp was established on part of the plateau in 1901.

News leaked out to the farmers of Larzac in 1970 that the Paris government intended to expand the camp to over twenty times its size, by closing 58 farms and restricting the activities of another 40. It was suggested that agriculture on the plateau was dying and that the remaining peasants were all elderly people. Neither claims were true.

Impressed by a neighbour, Lanzo del Vasto, himself a disciple of Gandhi, the peasants began what turned out to be a ten-year struggle to protect their land and farms. One hundred and three farmers united in a pledge never to sell. Many people from other parts of France came to support them, and to join in fasts which were shared by some of the bishops of the area. The peasants were careful, however, not to be exploited by other political groups who wanted to promote their own agendas.

Many of their actions were imaginative and humorous. In October 1972 they took 60 of their sheep to the Eiffel Tower in Paris and let them loose to graze on the grass of the Champs de Mars. They organised great tractor processions throughout the area and even towards Paris, to publicise their case. Without a permit they built a new sheepfold for 500 ewes on the plateau. They put back into production farms which had been seized by the military and even made their own

water connections when public supplies were refused.

The army became very uncomfortable not only with the confrontation with their fellow citizens but because those same citizens took every opportunity to dialogue with the soldiers. Many of the conscripts sympathised with them.

One visitor to Larzac during the struggle was François Mitterand. He turned out to be the key to change. When he was elected President in 1981 he cancelled the Larzac expansion scheme. Non-violence had triumphed. There had been only one casualty in the entire ten years despite tense confrontations. A bystander was blinded in one eye by a gas canister thrown by a gendarme.

Rosa Parks Who Would Not Be Moved

Mrs Rosa Parks lived in Montgomery, Alabama. She was a seamstress in a men's clothing store. After work on 1 December 1955 she got on to the bus as usual to go home. The law of the state was that a black person had to give up his or her seat if a white person wanted it. That evening a white man demanded her seat and the bus driver told her 'If you don't stand up I'm going to have you arrested'. Rosa Parks refused. Years of practical work for the National Association for the Advancement of Coloured People had prepared her for this moment. 'I am not going to move,' she said. She was at once arrested and so started a great campaign for racial justice which soon involved Martin Luther King, a young Baptist minister.

But it was Rosa Parks, by breaking the law, who started it all. The day after her arrest 50,000 people in Montgomery boycotted the buses. Many of them walked miles to work every day. The boycott lasted from December 1955 to December 1956 when at last the Supreme Court declared that the Alabama law was unconstitutional. Only then did Rosa Parks get on a Montgomery bus to find herself being driven by the same bus driver who a year before had ordered her out of her seat. This time he said nothing.

Hers was a brave action. As a child she remembered 'going to sleep . . . hearing the Klan ride at night and hearing a lynching . . .' Rosa Parks challenged the law in order to demand justice for black people. A small act of resistance was the seed from which grew a great campaign.

Franz Jägerstätter – Christian Martyr

Born in 1907, Franz Jägerstätter was the illegitimate son of an Austrian farmer's maid. His father was killed in the First World War.

Franz grew up in the little village of St Radegund and became a farmer like most of his contemporaries. He married in 1936 and in due course became the father of three small girls. He was one of the few who expressed public opposition to Hitler's takeover of Austria in 1938. Though he did serve in the army for a short training period at the start of the war, he was released to continue his work as a farmer.

Increasingly, however, he became convinced that Hitler's war was not a just one. His deep Christian convictions became more dangerous in view of the climate of oppression. Nevertheless he did not keep his anti-Nazi views to himself.

In 1943 he was called up again. This time he showed astonishing courage. He refused to take the unconditional military oath of obedience to the Fuhrer. Such obedience, he said, he owed only to Christ. He was at once imprisoned. His wife stood by him but his parish priest did his best to make him change his mind, to no avail.

Franz was court-martialled, sentenced to death, and finally beheaded in Brandenburg Prison on 9 August 1943. The prison chaplain told some nuns who lived near the prison that Franz was the only saint that he had ever met. After the war his ashes were brought back to St Radegund and buried next to the church of which he had once been the sacristan.

It took many years before his fellow villagers began to think of him as a hero rather than as an eccentric or even a traitor. But now, more than fifty years after his death, people from all over the world come to St Radegund on 9 August to honour his faith and courage. It is hoped that the Catholic Church will one day canonise him as a saint.

The unknown farmer has become an international hero to many who resist the demands of tyranny and militarism today.

ACTIVITY SHEET
Actions for Peace and Justice

Look through the list of peaceful events that you have drawn up between you and those on the Information Sheets. Try to match them to the headings given in this list. Then, discuss with other members of your group what you think the benefits and risks of each action are

(a) for those involved and,

(b) for the issue involved.

Protest and Persuasion

● writing letters

● signing petitions

● vigils or marches

● rallies or demonstrations

Non-Cooperation

● refusing to do military service

● refusing to buy from a certain place or country

● refusing to obey a law that you believe to be unjust

● refusing to pay some or all of your taxes

Intervention

● sit-ins

● blocking entrances to buildings or military sites

● putting yourself between people or groups trying to harm others

● occupying land that is being misused or damaged

Event	Benefit	Risks

12 ACTIVITY SHEET
Examples of Civil Disobedience

The following are examples of civil disobedience. Where would you draw the line? Read through the list and then tick 'yes' or 'no' according to which you approve of and which you do not.

1 Three people walk into a nuclear test site. They kneel down and begin to pray. The police arrest them for trespass.

2 A woman withholds from the Inland Revenue the portion of her taxes that would be spent on 'defence'. She is likely to go to prison as a result.

3 At night a group of peace protestors gain entry to a military aircraft that can carry nuclear weapons. They begin to disarm the aircraft before they are arrested.

4 A man refuses to pay his community tax because he feels it is an unjust tax. He goes to court to argue his case and has bailiffs sent to claim his property.

5 Members of a youth group build a 'cardboard city' outside the Department of Environment to protest the Government's housing policy. They refuse to move when asked to do so.

6 Five young women climb the wall into Buckingham Palace and unfurl a banner protesting Britain's testing of nuclear weapons on Native American land.

7 A group of protestors hold a vigil outside an Embassy of a country which violates the rights of its people. They burn the names of hundreds of people who have been killed.

	Yes	No		Yes	No
1			5		
2			6		
3			7		
4					

Definitions of Non-violence

Read through these statements and then work through the discussion points.

1 Non-violence is not a cover for cowardice, it is a virtue of the brave.

2 Non-violence should make people conscious of the real power within themselves. The moment people take responsibility for their lives, they begin to feel a kind of personal power.

3 The purpose of non-violence is not to repress or defeat but to convert or change the person seen as the 'enemy'.

4 At the centre of non-violence stands the principle of love. Along the way of life, someone must have sense enough and morality enough to cut off the chain of hate.

5 Non-violence is not only a way of acting, it is a way of thinking and living. It is important to show people that consistent non-violence is effective.

6 Non-violence is perhaps the most exacting of all forms of struggle, it excludes self-interest and demands first of all that one be ready to suffer evil and even the threat of death without violent retaliation.

Points for Discussion

a) What are the similarities and differences between your definition of non-violence and those given in the statements?

b) Which of the statements do you find most challenging and why?

c) From your discussion, can you come up with a group definition of non-violence?

3 Pressure Groups

Lesson One

AIM

To give insight into the way in which campaigns work and explain with some practical examples.

OBJECTIVE

To encourage students to explore their own ideas about the way in which peaceful protest can be conducted.

RESOURCES

Background reading on the life and work of Mahatma Gandhi and Martin Luther King Jr could be useful. The examples on Information Sheets 14–18 should be read before tackling the exercise below; Activity Sheet 19.

METHOD

1 Ask the class to read the examples on Information Sheets 14–18 and identify the range of methods used. This should include posters pictorially displaying the issue, information leaflets for the public, press releases for the media, actions such as boycotts, demonstrations, theatrical presentations etc.

2 Divide the students into groups of three or four and distribute Activity Sheet 19. Assign a scenario to each group and instruct them to devise a campaign which they feel they could all agree to do. Each group should appoint a spokesperson who would explain the strategy to the rest of the class.

Lesson Two

AIM

To explore the protest surrounding the Newbury bypass.

RESOURCE

Activity Sheet 20.

METHOD

1 Explain what a bypass is and why people want it built.

2 In groups, find reasons for and against building the bypass.

3 Work through the activities.

Rainforest Timber Protest: the Melbourne RAG Campaign, Australia

Rainforests are crucial to life on earth as they contain the richest and most complex ecosystems on the planet. Rainforests cover 2% of the earth's surface and each minute humans destroy 100 acres.

Australia imports over 200,000 cubic metres of rainforest timber each year. To draw attention to the role of Australia in rainforest destruction the Melbourne Rainforest Action Group (RAG) decided to blockade the Yarra river during the arrival of a rainforest timber ship. RAG includes all elements of a non-violent planning action group – research, negotiations, education and preparation. The group worked with the Waterside Workers Federation and the Seamans Union for support. Some were responsible for dealing with the media, others for communication within the group.

When the ship appeared on 13 April 1989 all the elements of non-violence were used: protest and persuasion, non-cooperation and non-violent intervention. Those by the water had banners and information to hand out to the press. The group itself sang songs. The union workers did not unload the ship for 24 hours and the river was blockaded by lots of canoes, small boats crafts and swimmers. 46 of the 200 people involved went into the water. Everyone involved had been told about their legal responsibilities and the likelihood of arrest. The whole event was videoed and interviews were given to the press immediately after the blockade. As a result of this action RAG has much broader support and fewer people buy items made from tropical hardwoods.

The French Government Announces It Is to Resume the Testing of Nuclear Weapons in the Pacific

On 14th June 1995 Jacques Chirac, President of France, announced that France was to resume nuclear testing in the 'French Pacific' in September 1995 after three years cessation. For the peace movement, this was a signal that the nuclear arms race was beginning again. In order for new nuclear weapons to be developed, they have to be tested. Consequently testing is an indicator that the nuclear weapons industry is creating more weapons.

Youth and Student CND (Campaign for Nuclear Disarmament) along with a coalition of other peace groups such as the National Peace Council and Campaign Against the Arms Trade got together to discuss their strategies.

Firstly they decided that we should all boycott French wine and they approached several wine suppliers to inform them of this. The national governments of Australia, New Zealand and South Africa condemned the announcement from the French and gave the campaigning groups some wine from their countries. The boycott later spread to other French products.

Each Tuesday a protest was made outside the French Embassy to make it clear that people did not want them to resume. On Bastille Day – 14.7.95 – a protest was created of One Hundred Marcel Marceaux – see Information Sheet 15.

On Sunday 16th July, 50 years since the first nuclear test, a mass rally was held in Trafalgar Square. People gathered with banners and leaflets to hear from speakers of a range of protesting groups, including other French peace groups. One Labour MP spoke and two people from Japan who survived the bomb being dropped in their region. A mass die in was held at 1.30 p.m. when the bells of St Martins-in-the Fields were rung 50 times to remember the horror of dropping the nuclear bomb on people.

The French Government tested nuclear weapons six times in all during the months following the demonstration. Although for some this was a great disappointment, for many in the peace movement, it was a reminder that we need to keep working together to challenge what we think is wrong. The testing was an opportunity for many people to think again about what we are doing to our planet and to each other by releasing poisons into the Pacific yet again.

NEWSDESK/PHOTODESK

Youth and Student

Campaign for Nuclear Disarmament

News Release

14.7.95

RE. NUCLEAR TESTS: "COMMITTEE OF ONE HUNDRED MARCEL MARCEAUX" TO TAKE PART IN BLOCKADE OF FRENCH EMBASSY

At 5–7.30pm today, Bastille Day (14/7/95) outside the French Embassy (58 Knightsbridge, SW1) one hundred Marcel Marceaux will take part in a protest at France's planned nuclear tests.

The protest marks one month exactly since Jacques Chirac made his announcement (on Tuesday 14/6/95 at 7.30pm). The month of growing global protest has included weekly Tuesday protests outside the French embassy in London, which have doubled in size each week.

Today's protest will also mark the official launch of a campaign of non-violent civil disobedience, as announced by Youth CND at Westminster Central Hall after the 1995 Aldermaston to London march (during the Non-Proliferation Treaty Conference). These actions will take place parallel to the weekly Tuesday protests.

Today's protest, which is being called by Youth CND in advance of the CND demonstration this Sunday, will include demonstrators dressed as the famous French mime artist Marcel Marceau, carrying placards with a humorous French Revolutionary theme.

A spokesperson for Youth CND, Eirlys Rhiannon, said today: "The world's choice is nuclear-free or nuclear free-for-all. But if more and more of us don't stand up and speak out, this new nuclear nightmare will become unstoppable."

> **Note to photodesk:**
> Photo opportunities – the Marcel Marceaux (dressed in black and white with white faces) carrying various humorous placards. TV/Video note the 7.30pm ceremonial ending below.
>
> **7.30pm – The 100 'Marcel Marceaux's silent sit-down blockade will end as in unison they ceremoniously stand up and "break the silence" as an example to others.**

50 Years Under the Bomb

'I am become death, the destroyer of worlds'

Robert Oppenheimer

ON 16 July 1945, at 5.29 am (1.29 pm BST), the world's first atomic explosion – the Trinity Test – took place in America's New Mexico desert. On 16 July 1995, CND is commemorating that beginning by demanding a ban on all nuclear weapons.

Nuclear weapons have cast a shadow over us all for far too long. The nuclear age has created many victims – the 200,000 people who died at Hiroshima and Nagasaki, the British service people suffering from cancer as a result of being present at nuclear tests in the 1950s, the native peoples of Australia, Nevada and the Pacific Islands, their lands devastated by testing.

Nuclear weapons also cost a phenomenal amount of money. Money which should have gone into the health service, education and the regeneration of industry, has instead been wasted on weapons too awful ever to be used.

We must turn away from nuclear weapons forever.

Join us on 16 July for music, readings, poetry and speeches from Japanese survivors of Hiroshima, victims of nuclear testing, MPs, church leaders and international peace activists. Join us and demand a global ban on nuclear weapons.

We need your help. Support the demand for a global ban! Now!

Sponsors include Greenpeace.

---

50 YEARS UNDER THE BOMB

Sunday 16 July '95

Time for a nuclear-free world

Trafalgar Square, London WC1. 1 to 4 pm

• **mass die-in** • **speeches** • **music** • **poetry**

Campaign for Nuclear Disarmament

Greenpeace and Brent Spar

On the 16th February 1995 the UK Government announced that it had given Shell permission to dump a large, heavily contaminated oil installation into the sea to the west of Scotland and Ireland. The Brent Spar oil storage installation contains over 100 tonnes of toxic sludge and more than 30 tonnes of radioactive materials which are a serious threat to the marine environment. After researching into the materials contained in Brent Spar, the options for disposal open to the UK Government and its international obligations not to pollute the environment, Greenpeace decided on a plan of action. (Greenpeace is an international organisation committed to standing up for what you believe in. It has worked on issues such as establishing a whale sanctuary, opposing nuclear testing, stopping the killing of baby seals.)

On 30th April 1995 four Greenpeace climbers scaled and took up residence on Brent Spar. They took food and equipment for what they thought might be a long time. A boat called the Moby Dick was nearby which was harassed by a Shell boat. From both the Moby Dick and Brent Spar, Greenpeace issued press statements about the potential destruction of the environment which would be caused by the dumping of the platform.

On 12th May a Shell helicopter landed on Brent Spar with two Sheriffs officers from Aberdeen who had a legal injunction. 'Shell's attempts to use the courts to enforce its disastrous plan to pollute the seas demonstrates its contempt for public concern about its operations, fishermen's livelihoods and for the health of the North Sea' (Chris Rose of Greenpeace). Photographs of the Sheriffs on the platform were made available to the international press. On 13th May international criticism of the plan to dump grew. Ritt Bjerregaard, EU Commissioner for the Environment, supported the Greenpeace action. The Danish Minister for Environment and Energy called for the sea not to be used as a dustbin. Meanwhile, Shell tried to get the courts to stop Greenpeace from issuing information to the press but were unsuccessful.

The occupation of the platform ended on 24th May and Greenpeace continued to send press releases about the situation. Pressure to change the Government plans increased in the UK from other countries and the Labour Party. By this time the battle was now in courts, in the event in Scottish courts. 'The decision, [to have the case heard in Scotland] based on a legal technicality, means that no British court can hear Greenpeace challenge the Government. In effect it is a decision by the UK Government to allow Shell to dump toxic chemicals and radioactive waste at sea' (Madeleine Cobbing of Greenpeace).

After much legal work and continued pressure on Shell and the UK Government, Shell made the following statement on 20th June 1995:

'Shell UK has decided to abandon deepwater disposal and seek from the UK authorities a licence for onshore disposal. This application for onshore disposal will include a further review of methods to minimise the risks involved.'

 **INFORMATION SHEET**
Campaign Against Animal Exports

In Britain there is an ongoing campaign against animal cruelty including the treatment of farm animals in meat and dairy production, the capture of animals for fur and the use of animals for testing drugs or diseases.

During the winter of 1994/1995 there was a dramatic increase in protests against the export of live animals from Britain to the continent. Animals are sent overseas as livestock to be killed on arrival to ensure that the meat is fresh. The animals are packed into lorries in layers on top of one another and loaded into ships along with other animals. Protestors gathered at ports to blockade the roads and stop the animals being loaded.

Sheep convoy beats blockade

by ADRIAN LEE

DISTRAUGHT animal lovers wept in frustration last night as two lorries loaded with 1,200 sheep broke through their port blockade.

Two thousand protesters had tried to block the convoy's route through Brightlingsea in Essex.

But police in riot gear swept them aside as the trucks inched forwards, breaching a law banning lorries from the town's streets after 11pm.

Inside one truck, sheep could be seen stacked three layers high.

Once inside the docks they joined another 1,000 animals already aboard the livestock carrier MV Caroline due to sail for Belgium at 2.30am.

Twenty-one demonstrators were arrested and eight others, one of them disabled, were injured in clashes with the police.

Kevin Williams, 37, said: "They went mad. I was hit in the mouth."

As town mayor Ric Morgan, who had led the protest, demanded an inquiry, police sources said the lorry ban was broken for "operational reasons".

Mr Morgan had earlier warned them: "Don't come through on the grounds of public safety. It's too dangerous."

The following is one protestor's account in the nation-wide campaign to prevent animal exports.

"We went to Brightlingsea on Monday 16th January. We had heard that about a thousand sheep were to be loaded on to a ship called the *Caroline* for transport to Belgium, a sea journey of some 7 or 8 hours in fairly heavy weather. Myself, Joan and a friend, Walter, arrived at the meeting point outside the Community Hall, to a cacophany of motor horns and whistles, at about 11.30 am. The hundred or so demonstrators already there were laughing and good humouredly joking with the scattering of policemen, in spite of the biting wind. Joan, determinedly holding aloft our placard "Quaker Concern for Animals, Ban Live Exports", was at once besieged by an army of photographers. We guessed we were in for a long day and had come prepared with sandwiches. We had been given to understand that the animals were to be loaded for sailing on the noon day tide. That deadline passed quickly and rumour had it that sailing would then take place at around midnight and the lorries would arrive at about three o'clock. By half past two the crowd had swelled to five or six hundred, some wheelchair bound, quite a lot of elderly Brightlingsea residents. At about three o'clock a smart green Range Rover attempted to make its way through the throng of people, now numbering nearly a thousand. Someone began to run down the road to try and identify the driver and then the cry went up "It's Otley". The crowd surged up the road after the vehicle which was apparently trying to get to the wharf. A number of demonstrators managed to get in front of the vehicle, bringing it to a halt. Then Richard Otley, farmer and exporter, was subjected to the protests of the crowd. The man inside just sat there unmoved. His motive for coming into the town at that time can only have been to provoke some kind of reaction from the Brightlingsea residents, to show them in a bad light in front of the media. I saw two fairly violent arrests after the Range Rover had been banged and scratched. This in no way satisfied Mr Otley who declared that the police did not protect him in the way he thought they should have done. The crowd would not let him pass and his arrogance in saying that nothing and no one was going to stop him from his quite legitimate export trade did nothing to improve the feelings of the demonstrators. He was, under police advice, made to retrace the way he had come to a point where he could leave the town.

At 4.30 pm, feeling chilled from the bitterly cold wind, we decided to go home. We later learned that one lorry that did turn up at 6.40 pm containing four hundred sheep was forced to turn back. One skirmish won but the battle must go on."

The woods which you used to play in as a child, which have wild flowers and grasses growing, are threatened with destruction. The plan to bypass your town with a new road cuts through the middle of this wood. Work has already begun and although you wish you had done more earlier on, you and some of your friends are angry about this.

What do you do to show you disapprove?
What are the risks in undertaking this?
What do you think you will achieve?

A group of young men from the British National Party regularly sell their racist newspaper at the local market which is a gathering place for people of many cultures. They often gather and shout racist abuse at passing people. You and your friends are angry about this.

What do you do to show you disapprove?
What are the risks in undertaking this?
What do you think you will achieve?

You have read about some recent research which has shown that a power station not far from your home is partly responsible for the early deaths of farm animals and may be responsible for deformed farm animals being born. Parents of disabled children born in the area are claiming that the pollution caused by the power station is the reason for the disability of their children. You and your friends, one of whom was born with only one eye, believe the research and find this very worrying.

What do you do to show you want the power station to look at what chemicals it is putting into the air and water?
What are the risks in undertaking this?
What do you think you will achieve?

You have relatives and friends in an Asian/African country and recently received a letter from your uncle explaining that your cousin had been arrested. He said that government security forces took him and a group of local young men to prison and they have not been seen since. Everyone is worried about these young men and fears for their safety.

What do you do to find out more? What organisations do you contact to give you assistance?
What are the risks in undertaking this?
What do you think you will achieve?

In the Path of the Bulldozer

Protestors tried to stop the Newbury bypass being built in the 1990s. Some live in trees and have even chained themselves to them! Some lie in the path of the bulldozers or chain themselves to digging equipment. Some of these protestors stay there in a camp all the time. Some visit for the odd day.

For the Bypass

Newbury has too much traffic passing through it. The bypass will ease congestion and make it more pleasant to live in the town.

Against the Bypass

The new road will cut through countryside that contains much wildlife and some rare plants. The wildlife includes:

- The Kingfisher
- The Reed Warbler
- The Dormouse
- The Sedge Warbler

The plants include the South Marsh Orchid, the Bog Asphodel, and the Greater Spearwort.

Who is Right?

Who comes first, wildlife or humans?

I Fill in the speech balloons with the views that both might have.

2 Write up a newspaper report, including an interview with someone on each side.

C · War

1 Pacifism

Lesson One

AIM

To explore the meaning of pacifism, and why some people feel strongly about this issue.

RESOURCES

Activity Sheets 21–23.

METHOD

1 Discuss what people would do to or think about someone who refused to hit back. After some discussion explain that some think it is just as bad to hit back as to hit out first of all. Both actions hurt. Talk about the feeling people have of a need to defend themselves. List all their reactions on the board.

2 Explain that some people are total pacifists, rejecting any use of force. Others are limited pacifists, accepting a police force, for example, but refusing to fight in a war. They are not cowards; they have several reasons. (Look at Activity Sheet 21 and decide which of these seem to be the most reasonable or powerful).

3 Read through Activity Sheet 22 with the conversation between a pacifist and his friend. Work out short role plays about a situation like this in groups.

4 Look at Activity Sheet 23. What are each of the pictures and slogans trying to say?

'I am a pacifist because . . .'

1 Life is sacred and precious. I do not believe in taking another person's life even if they threaten me.

2 My religion does not allow me to kill.

3 War does not solve anything, really. It causes massive amounts of suffering and leaves people defeated and angry.

4 Wars turn people into moving targets. Putting on the enemy's uniform dehumanises you . . . You do not know the soldiers firing at you, and really have no quarrel with them.

5 It's the leaders who want wars. Let them get onto the battlefield and fight it out! Most ordinary people want peace with each other.

Put these ideas into the order that you think shows the strongest argument at the top, and the weakest at the bottom.

Strongest	
Weakest	

Fred OK. So you're a pacifist. Say, you're driving a truck. You're on a narrow road with a sheer cliff on your side. There's a little girl sitting in the middle of the road. You're going too fast to stop. What would you do?

Joan I don't know. What would you do?

Fred I'm asking you. You're the pacifist.

Joan Yes, I know. All right, am I in control of the truck?

Fred Yes.

Joan How about if I honk my horn so she can get out of the way?

Fred She's too young to walk. And the horn doesn't work.

Joan I swerve around to the left of her since she's not going anywhere.

Fred No, there's been a landslide.

Joan Oh. Well then, I would try to drive the truck over the cliff and save the little girl.

Silence

Fred Well, say there's someone else in the truck with you. Then what?

Joan What's my decision have to do with my being a pacifist?

Fred There's two of you in the truck and only one little girl.

Joan Why are you so anxious to kill off all the pacifists?

Fred I'm not. I just want to know what you'd do if . . .

Joan If I was in a truck with a friend driving very fast on a one-lane road approaching a dangerous impasse where a ten-month old girl is sitting in the middle of the road with a landslide on one side of her and a sheer drop-off on the other.

Fred That's right.

Joan I would probably slam on the brakes, thus sending my friend through the windscreen, skid into the landslide, run over the little girl, sail off the cliff and plunge to my own death.

Fred You haven't answered my question. You're just trying to get out of it . . .

Joan No one knows what they'll do in a moment of crisis and hypothetical questions get hypothetical answers. You've made it impossible for me to come out of the situation without having killed one or more people. Then you say, 'Pacifism is a nice idea, but it won't work'. But that's not what bothers me. I'm thinking about how we put people through a training process so they'll find out the really good, efficient ways of killing. Nothing incidental like trucks and landslides. Just the opposite, really. You know, how to growl and yell, kill and crawl and jump out of airplanes. Real organised stuff.

Fred That's something entirely different.

Joan Sure. And don't you see it's much harder to look at, because it's real, and it's going on right now? Look. A general sticks a pin into a map. A week later a bunch of young boys are sweating it out in a jungle somewhere, shooting each other's arms and legs off, crying, praying and losing control of their bowels. Doesn't it seem stupid to you?

Fred Well, you're talking about war.

Joan Yes, I know. Doesn't it seem stupid?

Fred It's human nature to kill. Something you can't change.

Joan Is it? If it's natural to kill, why do men have to go into training to learn how?

There's violence in human nature, but there's also decency, love, kindness. Man organises, buys, sells, pushes violence. The non-violenter wants to organise the opposite side. That's all non-violence is – organised love.

Fred You're crazy.

Joan No doubt. Would you care to tell me the rest of the world is sane? Tell me that violence has been a great success for the past five thousand years, that the world is in fine shape, that wars have brought peace, understanding, democracy, and freedom to humankind and that killing each other has created an atmosphere of trust and hope.

Fred I still don't get the point of non-violence.

Joan The point of non-violence is to build a floor, a strong new floor, beneath which we can no longer sink. A platform which stands a few feet above napalm, torture, exploitation, poison gas, nuclear bombs, the works. Give man a decent place to stand. he's been wallowing around in human blood and vomit and burnt flesh, screaming how it's going to bring peace to the world. He sticks his head out of the hole for a minute and sees a bunch of people gathering together and trying to build a structure above ground in the fresh air. 'Nice idea, but not very practical', he shouts and slides back into the hole. It was the same kind of thing when man found out the world was round. He fought for years to have it remain flat, with every proof on hand that it was not flat at all.

Fred How are you going to build this practical structure?

Joan From the ground up. By studying, experimenting with every possible alternative to violence on every level. By learning how to say no to the nation-state, 'NO' to war taxes, 'NO' to military conscription, 'NO' to killing in general, 'YES' to co-operation, by starting new institutions which are based on the assumption that murder in any form is ruled out, by making and keeping in touch with non-violent contacts all over the world, by engaging ourselves at every possible chance in dialogue with people, groups, to try to change the consensus that it's OK to kill.

Fred It sounds real nice, but I don't think it can work.

Joan You are probably right. We probably don't have enough time. So far, we've been a glorious flop. The only thing that's been a worse flop than the organisation of non-violence has been the organisation of violence.

> What do you think of the points of view expressed here?

CO-OPERATION

Armaments don't give security

IS BETTER THAN CONFLICT

Published by Quaker Peace & Service
Friends House, Euston Road, London NW1 ☎ 071-387 3601

Published by Quaker Peace & Service
Friends House, Euston Road, London NW1 ☎ 01-387 3601

'World peace will come through the will of ordinary people like yourself.'

'Let us take the risks of peace upon ourselves, not impose the risks of war upon the world.'

> What are each of the pictures and slogans trying to say?

# Conscientious Objectors

AIM

To develop an understanding of the tradition and practice of conscientious objection.

OBJECTIVE

To have the students examine criteria and case studies of conscientious objection with a view of assessing its value in the process of peacemaking.

Lesson One

RESOURCES

Activity Sheet 24.

METHOD

1 Introduce the issue of conscientious objection during World War I and World War II and various attitudes to this by people at the time.

2 Give out Activity Sheet 24. Ask the students to imagine themselves in the situation described at the top of the sheet. List their responses and then go onto look at how conscientious objection became a choice for many.

3 To help students think through conscientious and thought-out reasons for objection ask them to give their responses to the form based on the Military Tribunal. Alternatively, organise this as a Tribunal in the classroom. Three students could form the Tribunal and a number of other students could be objectors. Once each has put their case they could be cross-examined by the wider group of students. The Tribunal could then make a judgement on each case.

Lesson Two

RESOURCES

Information Sheet 25.

METHOD

1 Recall the last session in which the students gave some of their own convictions about objecting in conscience to war.

2 Ask students to read through the account of William Harrison (1891–1971) on Information Sheet 25. William was in prison for almost three years as a consequence of his conscientious objection. Then, invite them to express in their own words William's reasons for objecting to military service.

3 Now read through the responses of people at the time to conscientious objectors on Information Sheet 25. Which of these do the students most agree with/least agree with. Invite the students to give their reasons.

4 Encourage some reflection on what the students consider to be the **roots** of anger towards CO's.

Lesson Three

RESOURCES

Information Sheet 26.

METHOD

1 Ask the students to read through the stories of Ivan Toms, Erik Larsens and Franklin Brandon on Information Sheet 26.

Discussion: What is their reaction to these case studies?

Do the students think that those who volunteer to be soldiers have a right to object in conscience to particular wars as was the case with Erik and Franklin?

What do the students feel to be the advantages and disadvantages of

a) conscription

b) volunteer armies?

How do these testimonies compare or contrast with the testimony of William Harrison?

2 To help the students explore the difference between total pacifism and selective forms of conscientious objection invite them to look through this list of options and make a note of the ones they would accept for themselves.

● I could not be involved in any use of violence or coercion against another person or support any organisation of the state that used such force e.g. the military or the police.

● I could not use any violence or coercion myself but I think we have to have an army and police force.

● I would be willing to fight in a war to protect my own country but I would not go to war for any other reason.

● I could not fight in any war myself but I think that war is sometimes necessary to protect the innocent and weak in society.

● I think that I could fight in a conventional war but I would refuse to cooperate if chemical or nuclear weapons were used or threatened.

In groups, ask the students to

a) give the **reasons** for what they would accept;

b) think about the **consequences** of their choice for themselves and for others.

24 ACTIVITY SHEET
Conscientious Objection in World War I and World War II

Imagine yourself in this situation.

You object to war. You've never hit anyone in your life. If you don't enlist, you know your family will be subjected to abuse from neighbours and school friends. Women will give you white feathers and your workmates will shun you. You could even be sent to prison. What do you do?

This was the situation of many young men during World War I and World War II. Conscription was introduced in both wars which meant that all men between 18 and 41 years of age had to enlist. Those who refused were known as **conscientious objectors** (CO's). Many were imprisoned as a result of their objection.

Conscientious objectors had to prove that their objection came from a **genuine conscientious conviction** which they had to prove before a military tribunal.

Here are some of the questions they would have had to answer. Read through these and then put yourself in a position of a CO and write your responses or arrange a classroom tribunal, with three people as members of the Tribunal and a number of others acting as conscientious objectors

Question

1 What is your objection to military service?
2 Do you object to the use of arms in any dispute whatever the circumstances and however just, in your opinion, the cause?
3 Would you be willing to join some branch of military service engaged not in the destruction but the saving of life? If not, state your reasons.
4 Are you a member of a religious body which says that none of its members can engage in military service?
5 Are you a member of any other group whose principals object to military service?
6 If you are not willing to undertake alternative military service (a non-combatant post) how do you reconcile enjoying the privileges of British citizenship with your objection?

25 INFORMATION SHEET
Conscientious Objection in the Past

This is the response of one man, William Harrison, to the Military Tribunal in World War I.

I object to military service because the end and aim of such service is to deprive other human beings of their right to live. If I, having a grudge against a fellow Englishman, was to take a knife and cut his throat you and all other sensible people **would** call it murder, and it would be murder. How then can it be anything else but murder for me to take a gun and slay some German mother's only son against whom I have no grudge? I cannot and I will not **commit** murder . . .

War inevitably means that the nations involved degenerate and become like brutes. This contention is supported by the facts of the present day. Love, mercy, pity, tenderness and forgiveness, things which our Master Jesus bids us to practise, are all gone. We have forgotten that they ever existed. We hear of German women starving and say 'serve them right'. German ships with men in them go to the bottom of the sea. We say 'best place for them'. 500,000 Germans are slaughtered and murdered at Verdun, and elsewhere, and we say 'very good'. We forget that all men are brothers with one God and Father. I love my country too dearly to assist it in coming to such a deplorable state.

In 1916 there were about 16,500 CO's in Britain, about 14,000 of these went before Tribunals. Less than 400 of these were granted absolute exemption. More than 6,000 CO's refused to accept the verdict of the Tribunal, they refused to carry out alternative work of 'national importance' because it would still help the war effort. Many who persistently refused were imprisoned. During World War I 24 CO's died in prison. During WW II about 60,000 men registered as CO's. Many of these men were sacked from their jobs and the public attitude towards them was often very hostile.

These are the responses of some people to conscientious objectors.

'Before the war, I agreed with them (conscientious objectors). But now I feel that they aren't men. When my husband and I go out with him wearing his uniform, I wonder what it must be like to be married to one of those men. You would think they'd want to slink around corners if they met anyone they knew.'

'Personally, I don't think CO's are given a fair run in as much as they are tested on educational merits. They think that only an educated man can have a conscience. It's ridiculous to suppose that only certain classes of people can have a conscience.'

'I'd shoot the lot of them. Isn't conscription in? If my boy's got to go why shouldn't they?'

'I am a broadminded person, but I think CO's should be horsewhipped. If they're living in this country, they should be willing to fight for it.'

INFORMATION SHEET 26
Contemporary Examples of Conscientious Objection

National Service into the army, known as conscription, is still common in many countries including France, Italy, Greece, Portugal, Spain, Germany, South Africa. Some countries allow alternative service if the grounds for objection to military service are accepted.

Other countries have re-introduced National Service when at a time of crisis. For example, during the Vietnam War The United States brought back conscription and during the Gulf War both the United States and Britain called on their reserve forces or territorial armies to supplement their military needs.

Here are some modern examples of young men who had had conscientious objections to joining the army or fighting in particular wars.

Case Study 1 South Africa

Military service in South Africa is compulsory. In 1984, the End Conscription Campaign was set up to press for a change in the law. It calls for the right for conscripts to choose not to serve in black townships or in Namibia.

Ivan Toms is a doctor and a committed Christian. He carried out military service in 1978/80 as a non-combatant. He was called up again in 1987, but this time decided to make a public stand. He presented himself for arrest at the Cape Town army headquarters. On March 3rd he was charged with *'refusing to report'*. His case went to trial. Among those giving defence evidence was a pastor from Namibia who listed over 600 official complaints of mistreatment of civilians in Namibia by the South African Defence Forces (SADF).

Extracts from Ivan Toms defence:

''I find myself in the same crisis of conscience as thousands of fellow conscripts who are unhappy about serving in the army . . . I have always tried to be true to my beliefs, especially since coming to a deep Christian commitment. The reality of the injustices in our country has convinced me of the impossibility of continuing with any form of service in the SADF . . .

''I unwillingly served two years in the SADF as a medical doctor in 1978–9. When I was sent to an operational area, I realised that to kill another person was impossible for me to reconcile with my conscience. When I worked in the Ciskie homeland I was told by a major in military intelligence that my role as doctor was to spy on my patients. The military authorities always thought of their needs and not the needs of those in the barren homelands . . .

''After my time in the SADF, I felt called to work in the squatter camp of Crossroads. At that time the community of 40,000 Africans had no permanent medical service and the health needs were massive. The government's reasons for not supplying a service was that they saw Crossroads as merely a temporary community. Yet in 1986 there were 130,000 people living there . . .

"I really do believe I have been doing true military service in my work in the poorest squatter areas of Greater Cape Town. This is the kind of service that I believe will help to build a South Africa that we can all be proud of . . . I am one of the many unhappy and unwilling conscripts who have to make very difficult choices. Some choose to go into exile. Some choose community service as religious pacifists. I have chosen prison. I hope that my stand will contribute to the pressure on the government to introduce constructive alternative national service for all conscripts."

Ivan was found guilty and was given a maximum prison sentence of 21 months. In 1990, following an appeal court hearing, it was decided that Ivan should not be sent back to prison. This follows a massive campaign, the *End Conscription Release Objectors* Campaign. With the change in government in South Africa conscription has been ended.

Case Study 2 The Gulf War

During the Gulf War in 1990 a number of men and women in the United States who were in the military or military reserve forces objected to serving in **this particular** war. Here are two stories.

Erik Larsens could have been sentenced to life in prison. Instead he served a six-month sentence. Here is an extract of his testimony.

"In April 1986 I joined the Marine Corps Reserves to defend the American dream, which first attracted my parents to this country in 1958. I emerged from boot camp three months later, a fully indoctrinated fighting machine willing to go anywhere in the world to defend the ideas and freedoms stated in the constitution of the United States.

I first became aware of the realities of US policies through student activists. They introduced me to alternative papers and books. I learned about a Central American history of US sponsored exploitative policies motivated by corporate and personal greed. 70,000 Salvadorans have been killed over the last ten years as a result of US policies. I realised that I could no longer blindly follow orders from my Commander, but that my actions were ultimately accountable to a higher authority – namely God.

My deeply-rooted moral convictions have led me to declare my objection to the escalation of tensions and seemingly inevitable war in the Middle East. It sickens me to hear Mr Bush (then President of the United States) announce that 40,000 of my fellow reservists and 80,000 of my active duty brothers and sisters are going to wage war in the Middle East to protect 'our American lifestyle'. Oil imports could be cut in half if a sound energy policy was in effect.

Our presence in the Middle East has destroyed any hope of any of us ever receiving a peace dividend. We are wasting more than 24 million dollars a day in Saudi Arabia while the school system is still in shambles, while homeless people still walk the streets and while criminals are still on the loose . . .

I will refuse orders to activate me into the regular marines. I will refuse orders to ship me to Saudi Arabia to defend our polluting, exploitative lifestyle. I will refuse to face another human being with a gas mask covering my face and my M16 drawn. I declare myself a conscientious objector. Here is my sea bag full of personal gear. Here is my gas mask. I will return them to the government, I no longer need them, I am no longer a marine."

Franklin Brandon was also a member of the US Marine Reserves. At the age of 24 he enlisted in the marines because the recruiter said he could receive financial benefits for college. During his training he was confronted with the reality of the job of the military. At the same time he was working as an emergency medical technician for an ambulance company. He had to face court-martial and a prison sentence.

"I find it difficult to write any update on my case knowing that war is in progress. I also find it difficult to decide in what capacity I must turn myself in to the Marine Corps officials. I have spoken to my lawyer today and he said he would like me to turn myself in to the federal court. I have two choices. The first is to be restricted to the base and work at making dog-tags and other office tasks. This I see (from past experience) as being in direct support of the Marine Corps "Mission", which is in direct conflict with my conscience. The other choice is to turn myself in and be confined at Great Lakes Naval Base, which is not an easy choice, because there is a good chance of being severely harassed by my jailers.

"In either choice I know I will be harassed . . . As usual, I consult my Bible for comfort and answers. One thing weighs heavy on my mind and that is President Bush's remarkable display of impatience. To the American people I say "Love your enemies! Do good to them! Lend to them! And don't be concerned about the fact that they won't repay." Saddam Hussein and George Bush, I pray both of you will stop this insanity called war, lay down your arms and study war no more. I think we all realise that if you have a person who initiates violence (Saddam Hussein) and you have someone (George Bush) who responds to this violence with violence, you don't have peace; you have total chaos (war)."

War Resisters' International

What point is this cartoon trying to make?
Why is Joe 'a threat to society'?

3 Defence

Lesson One

AIM

To explore the concept of defence and the role of militarism in society.

RESOURCES

Information Sheet 27.

METHOD

1 List any enemies that you have had in your life.

2 How did you, or could you have made these people friends? Is it sometimes very hard or impossible to make an enemy into a friend?

3 Look at the cartoon on Information Sheet 27. What is the inner struggle?

4 Read through, and discuss the material on defence and deterrence on Information Sheets 27, 28.

5 Imagine that you are the President of a developing country. Why might you want to get nuclear weapons? Make a list of four points.

6 How is deterrence used

    a) between countries

    b) in society

    c) in school

    d) between individuals?

Is this a good way of keeping peace? Are there any alternatives?

Defence

MADNESS!
TO FIGHT OUTSIDE OURSELVES
WHEN THE STRUGGLE IS WITHIN US

What struggle is going on within us?

'Every monarch keeps on a war footing all the troops which he might need in case his people were in danger of being exterminated, and this state of tension, of all against all, is called peace.'

Montesquieu

What is Defence?

The idea of **defence** depends on there being something to be defended and someone to defend that thing against (*a threat*). We might want to defend jobs from cuts, or defend our hospital from closure, for example, or we may wish to defend our country's interests in Europe or the world. The three branches of the armed forces in the UK see defence as the most important role they have:

> **The Royal Navy:** 'After our Falklands Victory, we must continue to patrol the South Atlantic to *defend* our interests in case of trouble.'
>
> **The Army:** 'Obviously the first duty of the Army is to *defend* our own country.'
>
> **The Royal Air Force:** '. . . commitment to keeping the peace, because *defence* is our primary job.'

Military Defence

Calling military usage 'defence' can be misleading. The same weapons and tactics used by the attacking forces are often used by the defending one.

Friend or Foe?

Defence relies on the idea of an *enemy*. It is a word which implies that others are likely to attack you. Labelling everyone in a country as an 'enemy' because we are told to by leaders and the media is obviously unfair. A 'nation' is a collection of individuals, each with different ideas and beliefs. Political leaders and the media can create an enemy overnight; this power is so great that a friend one month can be labelled an enemy the next. In the Second World War the former Soviet Union was a 'friend and ally', afterwards it became an 'enemy and threat'. Similar changes over the centuries have occurred in the way the British have viewed the Spanish, the French, the Americans, the Germans, the Japanese, the Argentinians and so on.

28 INFORMATION SHEET
Deterrence

One form of 'defence' is **'deterrence'**. This is the idea that if one country has the same number as or more weapons than another country, then this will frighten the other country from attacking them. Individual people tend to get along peacefully with each other – it is certainly rare to shoot one's neighbour because of a disagreement or argument. Except in places where there is a long history of violence, most people don't shop for guns and ammunition.

The Nuclear Deterrent

Humanity now has enough weapons to destroy all life on earth. The centuries old view that 'attack is the best form of defence' could lead to the end of the world as a habitable planet.

Many politicians and commentators say that nuclear weapons have kept the peace (between major powers) ever since the end of the Second World War. However, there have always been wars going on in this time, some of which, may be described as **proxy** wars.

Deterrence relied on two adversaries each having enough nuclear weapons to destroy the other's cities and industries; each being able to detect a hostile launch, but neither being able to prevent delivery of the other's weapons to their targets. If either side launched an attack, the other would launch its own weapons thereby achieving **Mutually Assured Destruction (MAD)**. Then the public was told that nuclear weapons were not there to be used, but to deter through mutual *threat* of use. This idea of deterrence did not allow for third-party nations to have or use nuclear weapons, or for any possibility of accident, whether caused by human or computer error.

> An involved example of a proxy war was the war in Angola in the 1970s. Three liberation movements fought for control of the country. Many of the troops – and most of the arms – were provided by the superpowers, USA and USSR, or their satellites. In effect, the conflict became one between 'East' and 'West'.

Military strategists were uncomfortable with a weapon the use of which was unthinkable. Thus, strategies were reformulated to make the use of nuclear weapons 'thinkable'. These weapons were made more 'accurate': it became possible to destroy missiles before they were even launched, or at least before they reached their target. MAD was no longer assured.

In addition, old enemies have become friends, and old friends, enemies. Despite treaties and agreements, increasing numbers of states now have their own nuclear capability or the potential to construct one. This includes countries such as Israel, India and North Korea.

④ Do We Need an Army?

Lesson One

AIM

To promote discussion on the themes of defence, deference, national assets and world crises.

RESOURCES

Information Sheet 29, paper, pens, dice.

METHOD

The following directions describe how to play a classroom game called *Powerplay*. It takes about an hour with students in four groups. There are three phases – national growth, crisis, outcome.

National Growth

1 Divide the class into four groups. Each student is then in the Cabinet of their group's country. Suggested names: Eurasia, Oceana, Atlantica, Slavica. One student in each group makes a UN style desk card with the country's name on it.

2 Give out the national characteristics slip to each country. They have to use these in discussions.

3 Give out the Trump card that they will use during the crisis phase.

4 Within each group choose two students to be Hawks and two to be Doves. (Hawks always go for an aggressive option: Doves for a peaceful option.)

5 Give out Asset cards. The groups fill in the details during stages 6–10.

6 Spin the dice to decide the population for each country. The result is the population in millions. This

information is entered on the Asset card.

7 Spin the dice again for each country to decide how much money they have. The result is their money in billions. This is entered on the Asset card.

8 Countries take it in turn to buy an army from the following options:

   a) 80% Superforce – £4 billion;

   b) 60% Strikeforce – £3 billion;

   c) 40% Standforce – £2 billion;

   d) 30% Token force – £1 billion.

   These are entered on the Asset cards, adjusting their finances accordingly.

9 Countries take it in turn to buy shares. The choice includes: Fighter aircraft; computers; oil; grain. A 60% share costs £2 billion, a 40% share £1 billion. There is an option not to buy. Their details are entered on the Asset card.

10 Their bank reserves are totalled on the Asset cards after all the dealing is over.

11 Make a scoreboard on the black/whiteboard with two columns, 'Country', and 'Score'.

Crisis

1 The groups take it in turns to challenge the others, e.g. Eurasia will say, 'Oceana, army!' If Oceana's army is less than Eurasia's, then Eurasia gains a point and Oceana lose a point. This happens for three complete rounds.

2 The crisis comes as the shares collapse. The spin of the dice decides which shares go to zero for each group, as follows:

1 = Fighter aircraft
2 = Computers
3 = Oil
4 = Grain
5 or 6 = Throw again.

Enter the new share value on the Asset card.

3 The groups discuss. They have the option of playing their Trump cards.

Outcome

Five more rounds of challenges are played during which time groups could play their trump cards. At the end of the fifth round, the country with the most points has won.

Points for discussion

1 Which countries today might fit the national characteristics on the cards?

2 Can you think of any wars started by an economic crisis?

3 A country might choose to use economic sanctions against another country. This means that there is no more trade with them. Do you think such sanctions are effective?

4 Did the team with a strong army feel secure? Do you think it is necessary to have a strong army? What would the alternatives be?

5 Can any country really afford to go it alone and ignore all the others?

6 Do you think the UN should become more active as a world army to maintain peace?

National Characteristics Cards

AGGRESSOR You will pick on and invade any weaker countries.	**ISOLATIONISTS** You will seek to help yourselves and ignore everyone else wherever possible.
DIPLOMATS You consider it your duty to defend a weaker country and help to stop war breaking out.	**PACIFISTS** You will only use economic threats.

Trump Cards

AGGRESSOR Invade the weak country. Take their UN title card. Their army reserves go to zero.	**ISOLATIONISTS** Close all borders. Play no further part in the game, but you score one point in each round.
DIPLOMATS Ally with a country. Combine all your resources and link your UN cards.	**PACIFISTS** Impose sanctions against a country. That country's bank reserves go to zero.

Asset Cards

ARMY –	POPULATION –
SHARE INTEREST % –	BANK RESERVES –

5 The Just War – Its Origin and Application Today

AIM

To introduce students to the history and use of the Just War Tradition.

OBJECTIVES

To become familiar with the Just War tradition and be able to analyse contemporary conflicts through the framework of the Just War principles.

RESOURCES

Activity Sheets 30, 32, 34, Information Sheets 31, 33.

Lesson One

METHOD

1 Introduce the topic.

2 Divide the class into groups of four and explain the ranking exercise on Activity Sheet 30. Allow about 20 minutes for this.

3 Bring the groups together and ask for responses from each group. Which statements were the most popular? From the responses, encourage discussion on the place of war in modern society. Is it inevitable, controllable or unnecessary?

4 Make a list of six points that would make the way a war is fought as fair as possible.

5 Ask the class to bring to the next lesson newspaper cuttings on stories about war or conflict.

Lesson Two

METHOD

1 Recall the discussion held in the last session as a means of introducing this session which will look at principles or guidance for the waging of war. Refer also to the lists of six points.

2 Divide the class into groups to look at the newspaper cuttings they have brought to the lesson (have some to spare for those who may have forgotten to bring them). Ask each group to choose two of the stories for further investigation.

3 Give out Information Sheet 31 and read through it with the class. Ask the students to read through their news story again and see whether or not it fits the guidelines from the Information Sheet. Each group to fill in their responses on Activity Sheet 32.

4 Each group then presents their story and responses to the rest of the class. How many of the present conflicts matched all or some of the criteria for a Just War? What do the responses tell us about modern war? Do they still have a role to play in the way we look at war?

5 Compare the points in the Just War tradition with their lists of six points.

Lesson Three

METHOD

1 Remind the class of the criteria for a Just War which they explored in the last session. Have Information Sheet 31 available again.

2 With the class, read through Information Sheet 33. Brainstorm with the students their views of the 'just' nature of this war, keeping in mind the criteria they have looked at. Allow about 10 minutes for this.

3 Divide the class into groups and ask each group to choose one element of the war – Air Attacks, Children or Sanctions. Each group has to prepare a case to present to the rest of the class saying why this example was or was not justifiable during the war.

4 Read through the alternative viewpoint 'Desert Storm Justified' Activity Sheet 34 and discuss.

'Just War'

> Read through these statements. Choose the one you most agree with and the one you least agree with. Share your choices and the reasons for them with your neighbour.

1 'The scale and horror of modern warfare, whether nuclear or not, make it totally unacceptable as a means of settling differences between nations'.

2 'There have always been wars, there will always be wars. There is no point in trying to control them, just let them happen and finish as quickly as possible'.

3 'It is up to the strong to defend the weak – whether at community, national or international level. That's the most important thing'.

4 'War begins in the minds of human beings. Since this is so, the minds of human beings must also be capable of ending war'.

5 'War is a crime against humanity. It is impossible to support any kind of war. We should do all we can to remove the causes of war'.

31 INFORMATION SHEET
The Just War Tradition

The Just War tradition has its origins in the 4th century AD in the work of St Augustine of Hippo. He was the first Christian theologian to attempt to provide a logical Christian justification for war. He regarded war as evil but argued that sometimes it was necessary to combat a greater evil.

St Augustine's ideas, along with those of St Thomas Aquinas in the 13th century, came to be known as the Just War Theory. The theory sets out a series of moral principals that must be strictly observed if war is to be justified. It was an attempt to limit the effects of war which is still considered to be evil. The theory is always developing.

For a war to be justifiable every one of the following principles must be met. (If even one principle is not met, then in theory the war cannot be justified.)

JUST CAUSE War can be fought only to defend against unjust aggression, to avenge wrongs or to avert evil. A nation can resist another in self-defence or come to the aid of a neighbouring country unjustly attacked.

LAWFUL AUTHORITY The decision to go to war can only be taken by legally constituted government or the reigning Sovereign.

RIGHT INTENTION Wars can only be waged for the right reasons. War cannot be waged out of revenge, or to humiliate a rival country, to intimidate and warn other nations by a display of power, to protect foreign investments or to satisfy a drive for domination.

LAST RESORT No war can be justified as long as there is any chance of resolving the conflict by discussion, negotiation or other non-violent action.

REASONABLE CHANCE OF SUCCESS One cannot go to war unless there is a very real chance that the reason for waging war can be achieved.

PROPORTIONALITY The 'good' achieved by war must not be overweighed by the evils that will result from war itself, such as loss of life and destruction of land, homes etc ...

DISCRIMINATION Military action must discriminate between military and civilian targets. Non-combatants must be immune from attack. Also, excessive violence, looting, massacre and torture of prisoners of war are forbidden.

In addition to these criteria as to whether or not to go to war there are also criteria or guidelines about the conduct of war.

NON-COMBATANTS Civilians must not be involved in direct attack and should not be the objects of military activity.

METHODS OF WARFARE Those must be lawful, reasonable and in line with international agreements. If one side uses 'illegal' methods, this does not justify retaliation using similar methods.

DISCRIMINATE USE OF WEAPONS Weapons must be aimed accurately at legitimate military targets. Indiscriminate attacks in areas containing non-combatants cannot be justified even on legitimate military targets.

32 ACTIVITY SHEET
Matching Modern War to Just War Criteria

Question   **Response**

What was the cause of the war?

_____

_____

_____

Who made the decision to go to war?

_____

What was the reason for going to war?

_____

_____

Could other means of settling the problem
have been used?

_____

_____

_____

_____

Has the war caused unnecessary killing and
violence?

_____

_____

_____

Were civilian lives lost in the war?

_____

What kind of weaponry/technology was
used?

_____

_____

_____

33 INFORMATION SHEET
Case Study: The Gulf War – Civilian Perspectives

On 29 November 1990, the United Nations' Security Council passed Resolution 678, authorising 'Member States co-operating with the Government of Kuwait . . . to use all necessary means . . . to restore international peace and security in the area'.

- The seeds of this war were sown many decades ago, but essentially its catalyst was the invasion of Kuwait by Iraq in August 1990. Others argue that the war would never have been fought if it had not been for the riches of oil in the area.

- No accurate figures exist of the number of civilian deaths during and as a direct result of the recent war in the Gulf. However, it is estimated that at least 100,000 people were killed during the war itself, and many more have died as a result of **economic sanctions**, damage to **infrastructure**, environmental damage, and **displacement** since.

Air Attacks

- First priority targets for air attacks were air defences, command and control systems, scud missile sites, air bases and nuclear and chemical facilities.

- Only 7% of more than 100,000 tons of bombs dropped on Kuwait and Iraq during the 40-odd days of air **bombardment** were 'smart' (electronically guided).

- An estimated 75% of all bombs dropped on Iraq missed their target.

- The second phase of air attacks specifically targeted civilian infrastructure, such as bridges, electricity plants and other essential services.

- Coalition bombardment effectively destroyed everything vital to human survival in Iraq – electricity, water, sewage systems, industry, agriculture and healthcare. Food warehouses, hospitals and markets were bombed.

- Damage to the sewage systems meant raw sewage backed up into streets and homes. Power shortages meant electronically driven water pumping stations ground to a halt. Water became scarce and what was available was contaminated. This resulted in epidemics of cholera and typhoid, killing thousands of children.

- In Kuwait itself, the loss of life was around 1,000. However, pollution of Kuwait's atmosphere and terrain, as a result of the lighting of oil wells may have long-lasting medical effects.

Children

- Tens of thousands of cluster bombs remain unexploded and partially buried in sand in and around Iraq's towns and cities. These bombs resemble 'an elongated cola can attached to a tiny parachute. Traction between the can and its parachute detonates the bomb electronically. When a child comes across one of these unexploded 'toys' and pulls on the parachute, he or she loses an arm or an eye, or more commonly a life'.

- Two Norwegian child psychologists, experts on the impact of conflict on children, interviewed 250 school-aged children to discover the effect of the Gulf War on them. They concluded that the children of Iraq are the 'most traumatised children of war ever studied.' Two-thirds of those interviewed believed that they would not survive to become adults.

Economic Sanctions

- As a result of the economic sanctions imposed on Iraq, food, medicines and other essential imports remained scarce and expensive.

- The world was told that food and medicine would be exempt from economic sanctions. From 6 August 1990 to mid-March 1991, it was illegal to import even a single scrap of food into Iraq – from any source.

- In early 1992, 30% of Iraqi children under the age of five (nearly one million) were malnourished. Shortages of baby milk caused an upsurge in infant deaths through malnutrition and disease.

Desert Storm Justified

In the Autumn of 1990 the world held its breath. Teenagers began to ask whether or not they would be called up. Ex-servicemen checked their release papers, the Territorial Army were put on standby to replace units in Germany, CNN established 24 hours coverage of the crisis area. Gulf War fever gripped the planet. Commentators and analysts considered the possibility of the conflict escalating beyond Hussein's act of aggression – capturing the small Gulf State of Kuwait and giving him direct access to the Persian Gulf. Would Israel retaliate for the scud missile attacks? If they retaliated would this split the Arab alliance and draw Egypt onto the Iraqi side? How would the Soviets respond to this? Many saw these as the first rumblings of Armageddon. The fact is that it was over within the year because the West had the technology, human resources, motivation and determination for a show of force – that put Saddam Hussein and any other prospective aggressor, in their place.

The best way to justify this show of force, Operation Desert Storm, is to look at the situation now, consider the costs, and relate these to the possible scenario had their not been such a show of force.

There have recently been elections in Iraq. Hussein has had to bow to pressure to retain some sort of mandate. Even African states are now holding multi-party elections, whereas Hussein's name was the only one on the ballot paper. His Government relies on tactics like this to remain in power. Too many failed promises, the biting of sanctions and the Kurdish problem have all weakened his position. His humiliating defeat by the Allies 5 years ago has made him and others like him, think twice about acts of territorial aggression to solve internal problems. Kuwait is free, the role of NATO as a world arbiter rather than Western security alliance is redefined and proven. The likes of Gadafi in Libya and Moi in Kenya know that aggression outside the bounds of UN resolutions will be dealt with by NATO. There is no oil crisis, world economies are stable. Iraq has no nuclear capability. There was no 'mother of all battles' because Iraq was not given the chance to fight it.

Undoubtedly Desert Storm contributed to this status quo. Had the West looked on as Iraq took Kuwait, the following scenario could have ensued:

● renewed conflict with Iran as tension mounted over territorial disputes around the strategic Shut al Arat Waterway;

● growing confidence and wealth within the Iraqi ruling party;

● instability in the oil prices and loss of confidence in money markets leading to an economic downturn potentially similar to the 1973 crisis;

● a dangerous power vacuum as the UN and NATO are seen to be powerless and unwilling to intervene;

● a growing nuclear threat from Iraq.

All this is speculation, but the facts justify the costs of Desert Storm. Financially Desert Storm was extremely cheap. Laser guided bombs, accurate reconnaissance and intelligence, precision bombing raids and covert operations meant that a 'surgical strike' was possible.

This throttled Iraq's military capability and cut their forces off from supplies, instructions, reinforcements, power and lowered their morale. Some civilian and military casualties ensued, but because of the technology available, and the co-ordinated efforts of NATO and the host Arab states, these casualties were kept to a minimum on both sides. Moreover, once the objective was reached, the UN mandate was not overrun, the Allies did not march on Bhagdad to topple Hussein and set up a puppet regime. Instead, the force was rapidly withdrawn and the situation defused.

In carrying out Desert Storm, the Allies were keeping to Aquinas' points for a justified war, although the motives were economic and political rather than religious. The status quo now is preferable to the possible scenario had Saddam Hussein been left unchecked. The end justified the means.

For discussion:

1   Describe what might have happened if Desert Storm had not been launched. List anything that might have been different in world politics.

2   Civilians were hurt in the missile and bombing raids on Iraq. In what way could it be said that the Desert Storm commanders tried to fight this aspect of the war as justly as possible?

3   Do you think the Gulf War can be described as a 'Just War'? Find a parallel for each of Aquinas' first points.

---

6 Militarism and Nationalism

Lesson One

AIM

To explore attitudes of loyalty, nationalism and the international human family.

RESOURCE

Activity Sheet 35.

METHOD

1 Introduce the topic using the material below.

Think of when you take your exams. How do you feel when you do well? How do you feel if other people do badly? Do you feel sorry for people who are not your friends but fail?

Think of your favourite team sport – netball, cricket, football, hockey.
How do you feel when your team wins? What is your attitude towards the losers?

Now imagine your country is at war. Does it feel the same supporting your country as it does supporting your sports team? Do you feel the same if your side wins in war as when your side wins in sport?
Do you feel sympathy towards the losers?
Do you feel proud of your country?
Do you have a side to support?

2 Imagine what it is like for women in a western country. What will they struggle to do? What might stop them?

3 Some people think that women are naturally more peaceful because they can be mothers – they carry and give birth to life. What do you think of this?

4 Read through the poem from Zagreb. What ideas are contained in this?

5 Compare the other poems. What ideas about war are contained in these?

Lesson Two

AIM

To investigate media bias and war reporting.

RESOURCES

Activity Sheet 36.

METHOD

1 Divide the class into groups of five to work through Activity Sheet 36.

2 Have a class discussion based on the group's responses.

Lesson Three

AIM

To explore aspects of nationalism and to introduce the virtues of international co-operation.

RESOURCES

Activity Sheets 37–40; music – Beatles *All you need is love*; Michael Jackson *Heal the World*; Bob Marley *One World*.

METHOD

1 Play the pieces of music. What ideas and feelings do these give? Are they too idealistic? Introduce the terms 'nationalism' and 'internationalism'.

2 Divide the class into four groups and give a different Activity Sheet to each one. They read through them, and discuss the questions at the end. NB Those given Activity Sheet 39 will need a copy of the UN Declaration of Human Rights.

3 Ask each group to prepare a short presentation on each Activity Sheet and to say what they have learned about 'nationalism' and 'internationalism'.

Lesson Four

AIM

To explore issues of patriotism and nationalism in the Falklands conflict.

RESOURCES

Information Sheet 41.

METHOD

1 In groups, write out a list of reasons why the Falkland's War happened. Could this have been avoided?

2 Do you think David Tinker's statement, 'all this killing that is going on over a flag' was justified?

3 Rewrite the *Stick This Up Your Junta!* headline from an anti-war perspective.

ACTIVITY SHEET
Militarism and Nationalism

Poem – written by women in Zagreb, Croatia

Out of lines
Means different colours
sounds
ways
Crossing the days
the thoughts
souls
Crossing every time
everyday
Crossing together
senseless war
Crossing history
So they put the lines
Words of women's future
Remind us
Remembering life in peace
Crossing the south and the north
the east and the west
Balkan
We walk across the earth
out of lines
when we see each other we know
we are together
When we think of each other
Miles far from
together
Remembering our dreams and goals
The wholeness
Despite lines and sides
senseless war
We are not alone
Imagine
out of lines

This poem was sent from women in Zagreb, Croatia to women in Belgrade, Serbia while their two countries were fighting each other in 1993. Serbia and Croatia were part of Yugoslavia until 1991.

1 Compare your reactions to the three poems on pages 63–4.
2 Do you think your attitudes towards war would be different if you were living in a country at war, such as the women in the first poem, or if you were fighting in a war, such as the men in the other poems?
3 How would you describe the different attitudes expressed in all the poems towards their country fighting?
4 Do you think that any of the poets is more patriotic about their country?
5 Do you think there is any distinction between feeling passionate about your country and its people?

The Soldier – by Rupert Brooke
If I should die, think only this of me:
That there's some corner of a foreign field
That is forever England. There shall be
In that rich earth a richer dust concealed;
A dust whom England bore, shaped, made aware,
Gave once her flowers to love, her ways to roam,
A body of England's breathing English air
Washed by the rivers, blest by suns of home

Rupert Brooke died in 1915 during the First World War.

Dulce et Decorum Est – by Wilfred Owen
If in some smothering dream you too could pace
Behind the wagon that we flung him in,
And watch the white eyes writhing in his face,
His hanging face like a devil's sick of sin;
If you could hear, at every jolt, the blood
Come gargling from froth-corrupted lungs,
Obscene as cancer, bitter as the cud
Of vile incurable sores on innocent tongues –
My friend you would not tell with such high zest
To children ardent for some desperate glory,
The old lie: dulce et decorum est
Pro patria mori.
(This translates as "It is a sweet and honourable thing to die for one's country")

Wilfred Owen was killed in France in 1918 during the last week of the First World War.

When countries go to war, their governments often censor news about the war. This means they may decide that journalists should not supply information about such things as troop movements, the accuracy of bombs and the level of opposition to the war in their own country. And sometimes journalists themselves decide not to report on certain elements of a wartime campaign. The argument used by both government and journalists is that it is 'not in the national interests to report the whole picture'. For example, a survey found that from the first deployment of US troops in August 1990 to January 1991, only 29 minutes out of 2855 minutes of Gulf news coverage, which was roughly one per cent, dealt with popular opposition to the Gulf build-up.

'A journalist has a duty to not tell the whole truth when a country is at war. This is to stop morale getting low.'

'If we live in a really free society, then we should be able to ask any questions we want to during a war, and be given truthful answers.'

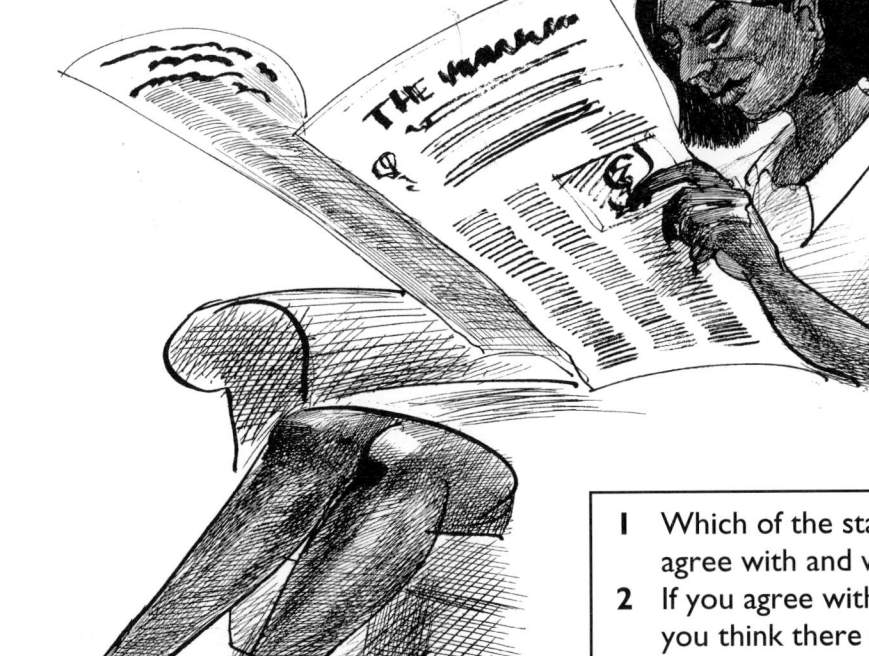

1 Which of the statements above do you agree with and why?
2 If you agree with the first statement do you think there are other situations in which journalists should not report all the facts?
3 Do you think journalists always have a responsibility to tell the truth?

This was said by the politician Ernest Bevin in 1947. The Americans had got the atomic bomb first, and dropped such weapons on Hiroshima and Nagasaki in Japan. The Russians were racing to get their own, followed by China. This was an age of 'Superpowers' – large, powerful nations. Britain thought of herself as still in this league after World War Two. The truth was that British influence was much less in the world than it had been, and much of the Empire had been lost. Politicians still felt that Britain had to have its own atomic bomb, or we would be left behind completely.

1. Do you think Britain was justified in getting atomic weapons? Why?
2. What do you think Ernest Bevin meant by his outburst about the Union Jack?

An old Rabbi once asked his pupils how you could tell when night had ended and the day had begun.

'Could it be when you can see an animal in the distance and tell whether it is a sheep or a dog?' asked one.

'No.' answered the rabbi.

'Is it when you can look at a tree in the distance and tell whether it's a fig tree or a peach tree?' asked another.

'No.' answered the rabbi.

'Then what is it?' his pupils demanded.

'It is when you can look on the face of any man or woman and see that it is your brother or sister. Because if you cannot see this, it is still night.'

(From the Hasidim)

I went on musing about why it was better and higher to love one's country, or town or village or house. Perhaps because it was larger. But then it would be still better to love one's continent, and best of all to love one's planet.

(From Rose Macaulay's *Towers of Trebizond*)

1   Why do people feel more loyalty to a country than a town? Why is it hard to love the planet more than your country? How would life change if people did this?
2   What sort of day and night was the rabbi talking about?

Ug and Uggo

Imagine that on a distant planet there are cities scattered around a vast landscape. Two of the neighbouring ones are called 'Ug' and 'Uggo'. Their citizens came from different parents and different parts of the world.

In each city, there are laws that must be followed. People are protected from crime, and they have their rights, all written up. But the citizens of a different city are not honoured in this way. They are strangers and visitors if they cross to another city. A city can be attacked and its citizens bombed and killed if another city feels threatened by it.

This is like our world, where nations give laws and rights to their citizens, but treat foreigners differently. We are all humans, and all should have the same human rights.

1	Why do we treat foreigners with suspicion?
2	Why should people of different races all have the same rights?
3	Draw up a list of four human rights that you think everyone should have. Then look at the UN Declaration of Human Rights to compare these ideas.

One Culture?

In many ways, people across the world are sharing the same culture. They watch programmes, use technology, eat fast food and listen to the same music no matter what place they come from. This creates a world culture. In what ways are the above things helping to create a world culture?

In some ways, this is good, as it is international. But local culture is suffering. Local food, crafts, styles of clothing or music are all important. These do not need to be lost if we become more international and less nationalistic.

---

1 Do you think we can maintain local culture if society becomes more international?
2 Think of some examples of your 'local culture'.

Case Study: The Falklands War

The Historical Claim

Two countries lay claim to the Falkland Islands – Argentina and Britain. It is argued by the Argentinians that at the time of the original claim to the islands they were uninhabited, and that they were since 'stolen' by the British. Since the 1950s the Malvinas (the Argentinian name for the Falklands) have been included in Argentinian school textbooks as being Argentinian territory. The British claim is based on continuous inhabitation of the islands since 1833 by English-speaking people of British descent.

On 2 April 1982 Argentinian armed forces occupy the Falkland Islands. Three days later a Royal Navy task force sets sail from Britain for the South Atlantic. The Falklands War is about to begin over the **sovereignty** of islands 400 miles off the coast of Argentina and about 8000 miles from Britain. The dispute over the island between Argentina and Britain has continued for many years.

The invasion and consequent response is seen by some to have been allowed to grow out of all proportion, as David Tinker, a Lieutenant in the Royal Navy who was killed during the conflict, reflects in a letter to his family:

> 'The most amusing thing is that it will be difficult to find the Falkland Islanders. With only 1,800 of them, there are, I suppose, 15,000 RN [Royal Navy] personnel, 4,000 army – 4,000 Argentinian army, and, say, 3,000 Argentinian navy: outnumbering the islanders by about twelve to one!'

Tinker was later to question the reasoning behind the entire conflict:

> 'I sometimes wonder if I am totally odd in that I utterly oppose all this killing that is going on over a flag'.

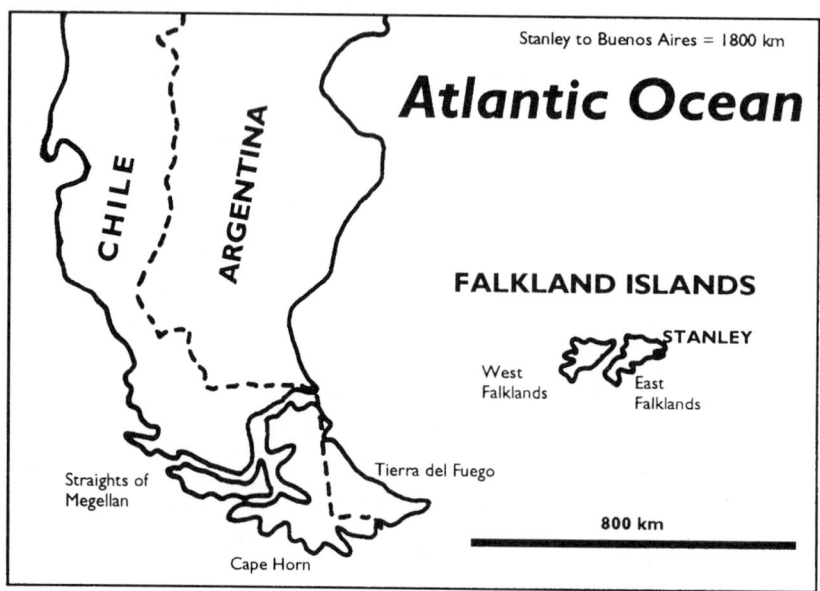

Stanley to Buenos Aires = 1800 km

Atlantic Ocean

CHILE

ARGENTINA

FALKLAND ISLANDS

West Falklands

East Falklands

STANLEY

Straights of Megellan

Tierra del Fuego

800 km

Cape Horn

By the end of the conflict 1,100 deaths had occurred, along with an unknown number of other casualties. Many of the Argentinian soldiers were young conscripts. The three Falklanders (the only civilian deaths) who were killed during the conflict were the victims of British weaponry.

The Media Story

As the task force sailed for the South Atlantic it took with it many reporters and broadcasters. These reporters, and those left behind, had to work under strict military censorship.

> *We Are All Falklanders Now*
> The national will to defend itself has to be cherished and replenished if it is to mean something in a dangerous and unpredictable world. (*The Times*, 5 April 1982)

Or if you prefer . . .

> *We'll Smash 'Em*
> 'Cheers as Navy sails for Revenge'. (*The Sun*, 6 April 1982)

The Sun was intent that Britain would not lose the Falklands to the 'Argies'; it was prepared to become the voice of a patriotic nation. Honour was at stake, and *The Sun* was prepared to ensure that the British public would not forget it.

Its campaign of patriotism included free badges bearing the slogan 'The Sun says Good Luck Lads', T-shirts, the inevitable Page 3 Girls and anti-Argentinian joke competitions. *The Sun* proudly declared itself 'The Paper that supports our Boys'. On 1 May 1982, it also included the following:

> *Stick This Up Your Junta!*
> A Sun Missile for Galtieri's gauchos
>
> The first missile to hit Galtieri's gauchos will come with love from the Sun.
>
> And just in case he doesn't get the message the weapon will have painted on the side 'Up yours, Galtieri' and will be signed by Tony Shaw, our man aboard HMS Invincible.
>
> The Sun – on behalf of all our millions of patriotic readers – has sponsored the

missile by paying towards HMS Invincible's victory party once the war is over.

The Sun was not alone in its patriotic fervour, although it had far and away cornered the market in extremes. *The Guardian*'s editorial of 5 April commented:

> The fleet sails now in restitution. The cause this time is a just one.

Later in the war, the *News of the World* was to print a scorecard:

> *Britain 6*
> (South Georgia, Two Airships, Three Warplanes)
> *Argentina 0*

In fact, it was the *Daily Mirror* that was to stand conspicuously alone, in not supporting military action, as its 5 April editorial showed:

> *Might isn't right*
> The islands don't matter. The people do. We should offer them the chance to settle here or anywhere else they choose and we should pay for it.
>
> What we must not do is promise to eject the invader, and then desert them at some later date.

But it was the sinking of the Argentinian cruiser, *General Belgrano*, that was to result in the most infamous headline of the war – GOTCHA! – *The Sun*'s editorial team's announcement of the sinking of the ship and consequent drowning of over 300 of its crew. Later editions of the same day carried the more subdued headline DID 1200 ARGIES DROWN?, but the damage had already been done, and GOTCHA! remains as symbolic of the media treatment of this war now, as it was then.

7. The Arms Trade

Lesson One

AIM

To introduce key aspects of arms trade history and patterns of trade.

RESOURCES

Activity Sheet 42, Information Sheet 43.

METHOD

This activity requires fairly good reading skills. It is a good homework exercise but may also be used in the classroom with the 14–18 age group.

1 Divide the group into pairs.

2 Give out Sheets 42, 43.
Allow thirty minutes for the crossword and thirty minutes for discussion.

3 Discussion: How do you explain the fact that opponents of the arms trade think the trade makes wars MORE likely and that the arms firms think it makes it LESS likely?
How do you think they would explain their arguments?
Find two reasons why the trade in arms increased and two reasons why the trade in arms decreased.

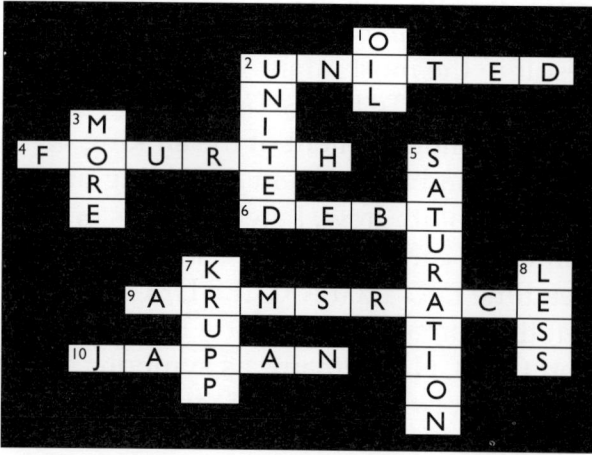

Lesson Two

AIMS

To illustrate the role of the British arms trade in the conflict in Indonesia. To investigate the personal effects of war on children.

RESOURCES

Information Sheet 44 (one copy of pp 78–9 per pair), Activity Sheet 45 (one each).

METHOD

This activity requires reasonably good reading ability as it uses primary sources written for an adult audience. Teachers need to ascertain whether there are any children in the group who would be upset by this activity – for instance those who have personal experiences of war, perhaps as refugees.

1 Divide the groups into pairs.

2 Ask the students to write down six things that freedom means to them.

3 Give out Information Sheet 44.

4 Give the students time to read the articles on the Information Sheet and then, **according to the letter and articles**, ask them to answer the questions below.

East Timor invaded Indonesia:
True/False

A third of the East Timor people have been killed by the Indonesian army:
True/False

The Foreign Office thinks that Britain should stop selling arms to Indonesia:
True/False

Indonesia is allowed to buy arms from Britain because the United

Nations says it has the right to self defence: **True/False**

The British Foreign Office says arms sales cause aggression:
True/False

The British Government does not care about human rights in East Timor:
True/False

British Aerospace does not export arms to the Indonesian government:
True/False

The British Government thinks Hawks will not be used against the civilian population:
True/False

The occupation of East Timor by Indonesia is illegal:
True/False

5 Get the group to go through their lists again, and cross out the freedoms which they think Amelia has been denied.

6 Hold a group discussion. What freedoms is Amelia being denied? Why? If Britain is selling arms to the Indonesian government and the government is using arms against the people in East Timor, is Britain in any way responsible for Amelia's plight? Bearing in mind that while the arms are made by a private company, British Aerospace, the government is responsible for granting the company an export licence to sell the goods abroad. Who, if either, is responsible?

An option at this point would be to write a letter from Amelia to the British Prime Minister.

1 Give out Activity Sheet 45.

2 Discuss with the students whether they think Amelia's letter would have any effect. Why? Why not?

For further information on Indonesia and East Timor contact TAPOL – The Indonesia Human Rights Campaign, 111 Northwood Road, Thornton Heath, Surrey, CR7 8HW.

Lesson Three

AIM

To encourage the students to discuss the complex issues surrounding the international arms trade, through dilemmas with which the students can identify.

RESOURCES

Activity Sheet 46, a copy of A or B per group, paper and pens.

METHOD

The moral dilemmas could be revised to take account of contemporary situations.

1 Divide the class into groups of three and assign EITHER Dilemma A or Dilemma B to each group.

2 Students discuss and write down answers to the questions on the Activity Sheet. Some will be writing letters, others will be writing down their views and the reasons for them.

3 Half the class could then explain their dilemma and their various solutions to the other half.

Lesson Four

AIM

To look at the effects of the arms trade on the arms-importing and arms-exporting countries.

RESOURCES

Activity Sheet 47 (one sheet per pair), overhead projector or whiteboard, pens, one pair of scissors per pair.

METHOD

1 Divide the group into pairs.

2 Write the following questions on an overhead projector or whiteboard.

   a) Why do countries buy arms?

   b) Why do countries sell arms?

   c) Does the arms trade ever cause any problems for the countries who BUY the arms? If so, what?

   d) Does the arms trade ever cause any problems for the countries who SELL the arms? If so, what?

3 Ask each pair to think of one answer for each question.

4 Ask each pair to suggest their answers to the teacher.

5 Give out a copy of Activity Sheet 47 to each pair and ask them to cut the sheet up into 15 cards.

6 Ask the students to match each card with the question that it helps to answer.

7 In pairs, ask the students to discuss the questions and their matching card(s) which they found particularly interesting and share this with the rest of the class in a final whole class discussion.

NB Some of the statements are not necessarily the 'right' answer. For example, President Saleh's statement could be seen as a problem

for Yemen, leaving it 'defenceless', a problem for the arms sellers who won't have a market if everyone follows Yemen's lead; or not a problem at all but a positive act towards real security and confidence building.

The statements have been taken from direct written quotations. The original quotations often used language which was too complex for students so they have been reworded for clarity. The sense of the statement has been retained. The statements originate from quotations from:

1 Stephanie Koorey, Trust for Research and Education on The Arms Trade.

2 Hemachandra Basappa, Documentation Centre for Disarmament Information, Bangalore, India.

3 Dr Chris Smith, University of Sussex.

4 Statement on the Defence Estimates, Ministry of Defence, 1993.

5 Campaign Against Arms Trade.

6 Stephanie Koorey.

7 Hemachandra Basappa.

8 Ruth Sivard, World Social and Military Expenditures, 1989.

9 Sir Anthony Parsons, former UK Ambassador to the United Nations and Iran.

10 President Saleh of Yemen.

11 Wade Tidbury, Falklands War veteran.

12 Institution of Professionals, Managers and Scientists, Manufacturing, Science and Finance and Transport and General Workers Unions.

13 UK Defence Statistics, Ministry of Defence, 1993.

14 Stockholm International Peace Research Institute.

15 Anthony Sampson, author and journalist.

ACTIVITY SHEET
The Ins and Outs of the Arms Trade

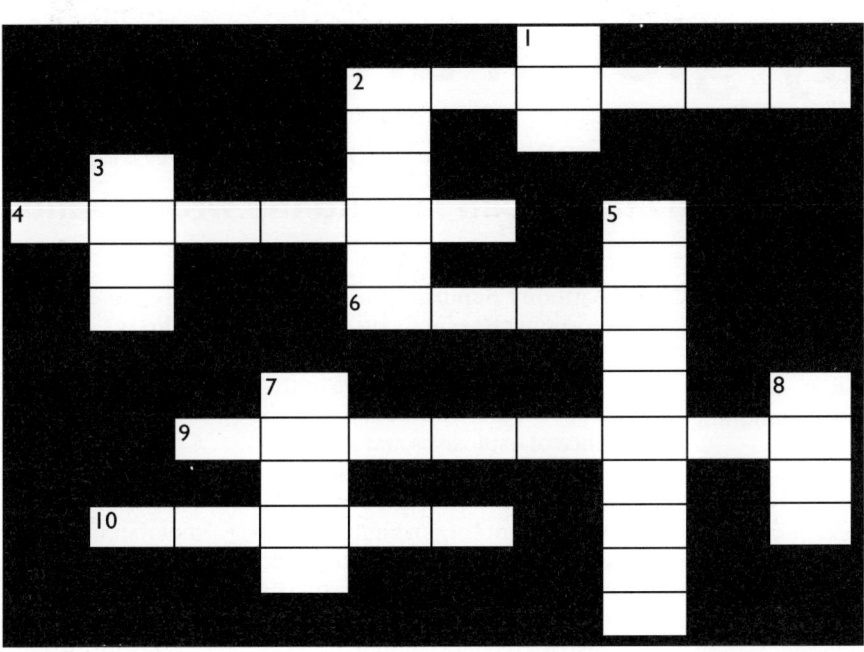

Clues

Across

2 One of the major reasons for the increase in production and sale of arms was the hostility between the Soviet Union and the . . . States (6)

4 Afghanistan was the . . . biggest importer of arms in 1991 (6)

6 One of the main reasons why Southern countries have had to cut their spending on arms was because of massive . . . (4)

9 In the two decades before the Second World War, some European countries rapidly built up their stock of arms. This is called an . . . . . . (4, 4)

10 This country was the seventh biggest importer of arms in 1991 (5)

Down

1 The increase in the price of this in the 1970s meant that exporters of this product, particularly in the Middle East, could afford the very best weapons (3)

2 The League of Nations was the forerunner of the international organisation called the . . . Nations (6)

3 Opponents of the arms trade argue that the increase in the availability and destructive power of weapons makes war . . . likely (4)

5 Another reason why there is a decline in the sale of arms is that there were so many sales in the 1970s and 1980s that many countries got all the weapons they wanted – this is called '. . . point' (10)

7 What was the name of the big German arms company that expanded in the nineteenth century? (5)

8 Arms firms justify the arms trade by arguing that the increase in the destructive potential of their weapons would make war . . . likely (4)

Deadly global arms jamboree

There is increasing unease about how certain weapons on the international market can fall into the wrong hands.

RECENT revelations about the sale of British arms to Iraq in the run-up to the Gulf War have led to fresh controversy in the UK about the morality of the arms trade.

Michael Heseltine, the Trade and Industry Secretary, said last week that Britain was responsible for only 2 per cent of Iraq's military build-up under Saddam Hussein.

The fact is the United Nations forces involved in Operation Desert Storm to free Kuwait were confronting Iraqi troops equipped with important Western wea-ponry, such as French F-1 fighter aircraft and long-range South African guns. This has led to fresh attempts to control the flow of arms.

Next April, the UN will establish a register of arms transfers — the movement of weapons from one country to another — during 1992. The information will be made publicly available.

This register will not cover all arms deals and will not put a block on sales. Yet it reflects growing concern that the international arms trade — worth £100 billion in the five years to 1991 — allowed sophisticated weapons systems to fall into the hands of dictators such as Saddam Hussein.

The UN initiative is by no means original. Anxieties have been ex-pressed about the power and the ethics of military sales ever since the growing pace of industrialisation prompted the growth of the modern armaments business in the mid-19th century.

Anthony Sampson, in his book The Arms Bazaar, says that the industry was "inspired and pressed forward by a handful of inventive entrepreneurs who developed the science of explosives and guns.

"Two characteristics were very striking from the start. Firstly, the development of armaments was regarded as inseparable from the whole movement of industrial progress. Secondly, it was of all industries the most global."

In the late 19th century the development of products such as hardened steel and dynamite, together with the spread of mass-production techniques, helped arms companies flourish. Among the biggest were Krupp in Germany and Vickers in the UK.

Yet the new firms found that they could not prosper simply by selling arms to their own governments. They began to look for markets overseas for their surplus goods.

Arms firms justified the trade by arguing that the increase in the destructive potential of their weapons would make war less, rather than more, likely. However, this argument proved less convincing after the great destruction of the first world war (1914–18). The war led to the first large-scale modern attempt to curb sales of arms.

In the two decades before the war, the leading European powers had rapidly built up their stocks of weapons. This so-called "arms race" was seen as one reason for the outbreak of war. In addition, the French, British and German

governments had found that the weapons sold by their domestic firms were now in hostile hands.

This reaction against the arms trade was expressed in the Covenant of the League of Nations, a forerunner of the UN. The document said: "The members of the League agree that the manufacture by private enterprise of munitions and implements of war is open to grave objections."

Despite these misgivings, little was done to stop the export of arms, either after the first world war or the second world war (1939–45). One factor was the success of the armaments firms in putting pressure on their governments.

First, they have employed large numbers of people. The latest Government estimates suggest that 150,000 jobs in the UK are linked directly or indirectly to arms exports.

Second, the companies have argued that although developing new weapons systems is expensive, one way of keeping down the cost of each new tank or plane is to produce large quantities. This is known as "economy of scale". Firms then sell the excess goods on the world market, giving their governments a twin benefit: cheaper defence and increased export earnings.

This has been the background to the spread of arms since the mid-1940s. In the immediate post-war period, Western firms with stockpiles of excess goods after Germany's defeat merely sold them to any willing buyer. But gradually, the process became far more complex. One reason was the hostility between the two superpowers of the post-war era – the United States and the Soviet Union.

Both countries developed new ranges of ever-more advanced weaponry, which they were quite happy to export to friendly governments as a means of increasing their global influence. Between 1971 and 1988 the two countries between them produced two out of three weapons that were exported, or "transferred".

A second cause of the spread of modern weapons was the increase in the price of oil in the 1970s. This allowed oil-exporting countries, particularly in the Middle East, to afford the very best that Western firms could supply.

For a number of reasons, arms transfers have declined in recent years. As the "cold war" between the main superpowers has ended, they have cut their own defence budgets and supplied fewer arms to their allies. Developing countries have massive debts and either cannot afford to buy expensive weapons systems or prefer to build them themselves.

In addition, sales in the late 1970s and early 1980s were so extensive that many countries have now reached saturation point.

Fighting for food

THE arms trade is closely linked to famine. Every big famine in recent years has taken place in a war zone, such as Ethiopia and Mozambique. Weapons from the US, the former USSR and Liberia are being used in Somalia's civil war. According to local reports, Soviet-made AK-47 rifles can be bought there for £54 — the price of 1,400 loaves of bread. In Sudan, the Iranian government has been arming Islamic forces against the Christian south of the country. As well as diverting resources, the availability of arms hampers relief efforts.

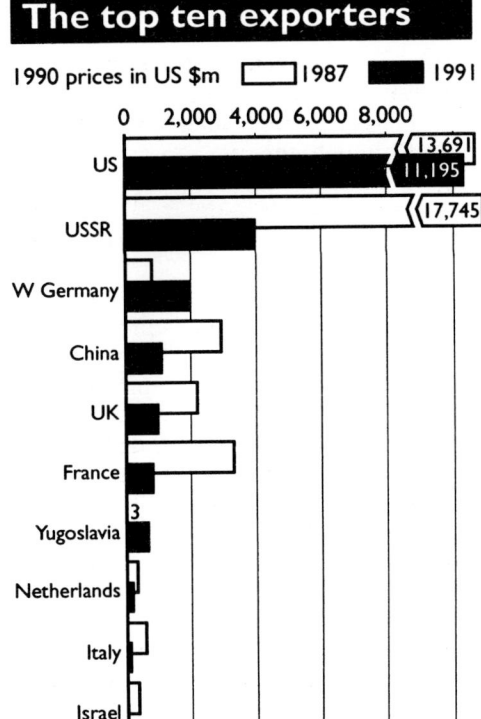

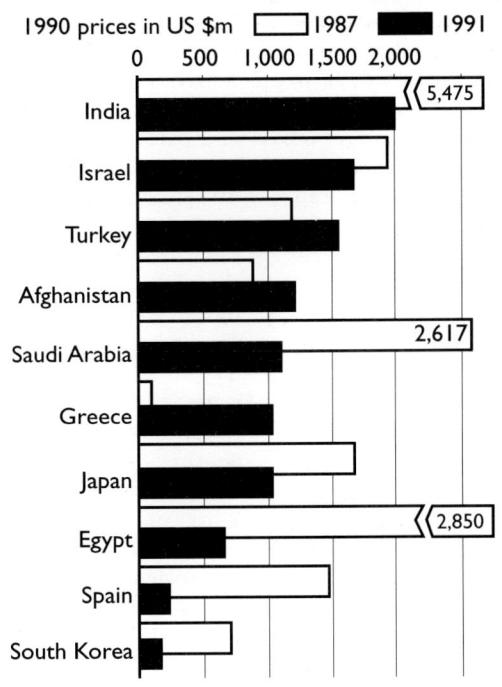

Education Guardian, 1.12.92.

INFORMATION SHEET
Secret Killing
Rights of War – Indonesia

FOR the children of the orphanage outside Dili, the scrappy little town which serves as the capital of occupied East Timor, the jungle is a nightmare.

'They told how they slept by day and ran, ran, ran by night,' said a young woman who cares for them, 'sometimes stepping on the squelching bodies of the wounded who had to be left to die.'

'I committed a terrible mistake one morning,' said the woman, whom I shall call Maria Jose. 'I thought we'd play hide and seek to amuse the children. Amelia, aged five, and I hid from the matron. I told her to keep quiet and not move a muscle. But she thought she was back in the jungle and on the run again. She started screaming and sobbing. It took me an hour to calm her down again.'

The horrors of a war of extermination bite deep into the memories of children, especially those who have fled into the forest with their parents to escape the Indonesians. But East Timor is an entire country in shock. After 15 years of occupation by Indonesian troops and deaths of perhaps 200,000 people, one-third of the Timorese population, 60-year-olds are resigned to a life of terror, five-year-olds are petrified. The young, however, are frightened — but defiant.

The Observer 7.4.91

British Aerospace (BAe) is Britain's largest arms company. From 1985 to 1991, BAe was Europe's biggest arms producer. Although the company manufactures various civilian goods like airliners and cars, military equipment accounts for around 40% of its total production. The company specialises in the manufacture of missiles and military aircraft such as the Hawk ground attack craft and the Tornado jet fighter.

In 1992 BAe's annual turnover was almost £10 billion and employees in the company's military divisions totalled 40,000, although these figures are both less than previous years. Arms exports accounted for 75% of the company's military business in 1992 and Indonesia is one of its best customers.

Arms deals between BAe and Indonesia in recent years include 24 Hawk trainer/fighter aircraft, Rapier missiles and Sea Wolf missile launchers. These contracts amount to many thousands of pounds. Other British companies such as Plessey and Ferranti have sold radar sensors and laser equipment, and shipbuilder Vosper Thornycroft re-equipped three frigates for the navy. The Indonesian army also has armoured cars made by the British firms Alvis and Daimler.

Foreign & Commonwealth Office
London SW1A 2AH
From the Ministry of State

11 January 1992
Alan Meale Esq MP
House of Commons
London
SW1A 0AA

Dear Alan

Thank you for your letter of 6 January to Douglas Hurd in which you refer to the concerns of a constituent about defence exports and military training for Indonesia. I am replying as Minister responsible for South East Asia.

As regards the export of defence equipment, our policy is based on respect for the rights of other countries, as sovereign states, to their own self defence under Article 51 of the UN Charter. This is a right we claim for ourselves and it would be inconsistent and discriminatory to deny it to others. All applications for export licences are, nonetheless, subject to strict controls and are scrutinised on a case by case basis. Importance is attached to the human rights record of the recipient nation and, if we believe a prospective purchase is likely to be used against a civilian population, the application is rejected. Obviously, not all equipment falls into this category and consequently we do not believe a total arms embargo on Indonesia is necessary. You refer specifically to the proposed sale of Hawk aircraft. We have sold Hawks to Indonesia in the past and have seen no evidence that they were ever armed let alone used against civilians. We believe it is improbable that any sold in future would be so deployed.

Similarly, we do not consider it necessary to stop providing training for members of Indonesia's armed forces. Such training is intended to improve competence and discipline and, by introduction to our principles and values, we hope that awareness of the importance of good government, democracy, and respect for human rights will also be increased.

Yours ever
Alastair

ALASTAIR GOODLAD

Dear Prime Minister

46 ACTIVITY SHEET
Moral Dilemmas

A   After months of job hunting you have been recruited by a company which organises exhibitions and trade fairs. The company will put you on a management training scheme and pay you a very good salary. However, you discover that one of the first exhibitions you will be involved in is a military equipment trade fair. British companies will be displaying their military products to representatives from foreign governments and armed forces. For example, there will be representatives from Pakistan, a country which struggles to provide its population with adequate health, education and food – yet they spend more money on their armed forces than any of these.

> **1**   Do you take the job? If yes, go to a). If no go to b).
>
>   **a)**   Did you have any reservations about taking the job? If yes, go to c). If no, go to d).
>
>   **b)**   How will you explain your reasons? Working on your own, compose a letter to the company.
>
>   **c)**   Is there anything you could do to express your views before you take the job or is there anything you would want to do after you had joined the company? Describe what you would do.
>
>   **d)**   Do you think there would be anyone who would consider turning the job down? What might be their reasons? Why do you think it is all right to take the job?

B   You have been offered a job as a trainee computer programmer with Vickers. Vickers makes the FMC Mark 5 tank and is trying to sell these to Indonesia. Indonesia invaded a neighbouring country – East Timor – in 1975 and has been condemned by the United Nations for human rights abuses. Over 200,000 East Timorese people have died as a result of the occupation.

> **1**   Do you take the job? YES/NO. Give your reasons.
>
> **2**   Would the decision be different if the following factors were changed:
>
>   **a)**   The company is not Vickers, but a small electronics firm called B-Royd. It does not sell tanks but it has sold a piece of equipment called a tracking device. It is possible to use these for military OR non-military purposes (e.g. guided missile systems Or telephone lines).
>
>   **b)**   Vickers no longer tries to sell to Indonesia, but has started negotiations to sell the tanks to India, a member of the Commonwealth which has long-standing ties with Britain. Indian representatives have insisted that it needs these tanks to defend itself against neighbouring countries like Pakistan and China which are threatening to attack it.
>
> **3**   Study the three statements below. Which one do you agree with? Explain your answer.
>   **a)**   Arms trading is never wrong.
>   **b)**   Arms trading is sometimes wrong. (When?)
>   **c)**   Arms trading is always wrong.

47 ACTIVITY SHEET
Counting the Cost

1 The South West region of the UK relies heavily on companies who produce arms. In 1991, 155,000 jobs were said to be dependent on arms production. Because of the cuts in spending on arms by the year 2000, at least 4,000 of those jobs will be lost.

2 One of the reasons why India buys arms could be because it is trying to prove to the world at large that it is a strong and powerful nation. Arms are a kind of status symbol.

3 The Indian economy is in ruins, inflation is high . . . and it will take years for the economy to recover. While there is no single reason for this, enormous spending on arms is partly responsible.

4 The sale of arms helps to maintain good relationships with friendly countries.

5 Both India and Pakistan have made it clear that their shopping lists for arms are based on what each thinks the other is buying.

6 The British government puts a great deal of effort into promoting arms to overseas buyers. The Defence Export Services Organisation (DESO) is part of the British Ministry of Defence. It has 10 overseas offices and 250 staff and exists purely to help sell arms abroad.

7 The incentive to leaders of Southern countries is the huge profits to be made from the production and sale of arms. Labour costs are very low and the overall cost of making the weapons would be less than companies working in Northern countries could manage. Southern countries could therefore sell their arms more cheaply than Northern countries could.

8

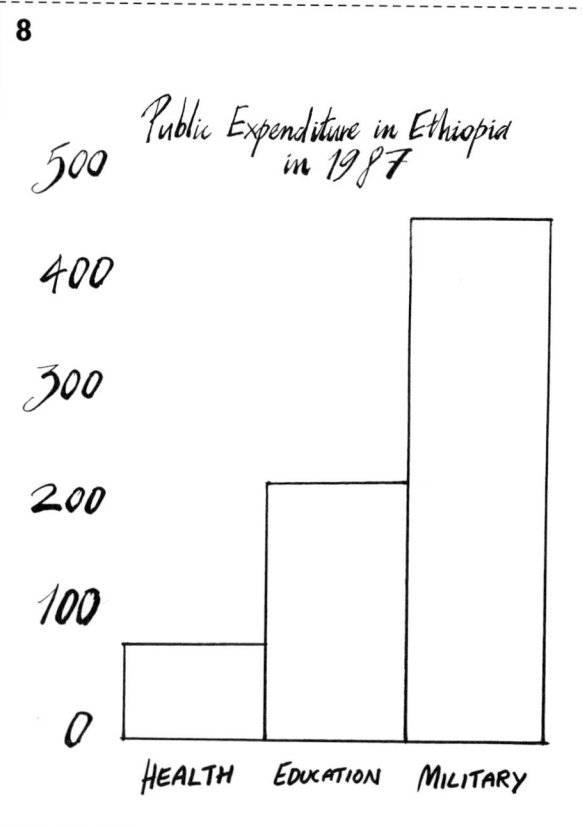

Public Expenditure in Ethiopia in 1987

9 Conflict in the Middle East has been made far worse by the sale of weapons to Middle Eastern countries by others, including Britain.

10 We have decided to freeze arms contracts because we as a nation want peace and stability. Both territories were spending millions of dollars to arm themselves against each other.

11 When I was a sailor in the Falklands, my girlfriend wrote to me saying how much overtime she was doing at her job in an arms factory . . . the idea that someone I knew was making something which was being exported and used to kill me shows up the horrors of the arms trade.

12 Civilian manufacturing in the UK has suffered from lack of investment, resulting in massive economic problems.

13 In 1992, the total value of arms exports from the UK was £1,506 million.

14 The global arms market has shrunk dramatically since the end of the Cold War. The arms sales of the world's 100 largest arms producing companies fell by 7% from 1990 to 1991.

15 For any nation faced with sudden wealth, arms provided the easiest and quickest way to spend money. Hospitals and schools create social disruption, while arms companies bring their own machinery and expertise.

8 Refugees

AIM

To give students an overall picture of what refugees are, how they come to be refugees and which areas of the world have large populations of refugees.

OBJECTIVES

To inform students about the worldwide distribution of refugees and encourage empathy with those who have been forced to leave their homes and become refugees.

RESOURCES

Pens, paper.

Lesson One

METHOD

1 Announce to the class that there has been warning of a massive flood and that they all will have to leave home and travel to safer ground. There is only transport for elderly people and school children will have to carry their own belongings. Ask them to write lists of what they would take with them, bearing in mind they must carry it on their backs.

They do not know when they might be allowed home. They do not know whether any provision has been made for them on 'safe ground'.

2 In groups of 5 ask them to combine their lists and try and agree on some basic items. Ask a spokesperson from each group of 5 to explain to the whole class why they chose their items.

Lesson Two

RESOURCES

Information Sheet 48.

METHOD

The United Nations definition of a refugee is '. . . owing to a well-founded fear of being persecuted for reasons of race, religion, nationality, membership of a particular social group or political opinion, is outside the country of his/her nationality and is unable or, owing to such fear, is unwilling to avail himself of the protection of that country'. (UN Convention Relating to the Status of Refugees 1951.)

One of the difficulties in the country for refugees and asylum seekers is proving to the British authorities that they have been 'persecuted'.

1 Using Information Sheet 48 (From *We left because we had to*, The Refugee Council) in pairs decide which are being persecuted or not.

2 Divide the class into groups of 4/5 and give each one a different subject from the UN list e.g. race, religion, nationality etc. and ask them to list all the things that they would consider to be types of persecution based on their subject. Report to the class.

Thousands of Kurdish men, women and children, now living in camps in Turkey, give accurate accounts of the chemical weapons attacks.

The Kurds were the victims of the Iran/Iraq War. They were not directly attacked by the Iraqi army.

There is a long history of conflict between the Kurds and the Iraqi government.

An Iraqi doctor says that the burns do not provide conclusive evidence that the children have suffered from chemical weapons attacks.

Iranian TV film shows chemical weapons attacks, with people dead and dying.

If they say that chemical weapons have been used against them, Kurds will gain sympathy from other countries. This may help them get their homeland.

Soil samples tested in Britain show that 'mustard gas' has been used. Mustard is a chemical weapon.

In the United Nations the Iraqi delegation deny having chemical weapons.

Kurdish guerrillas report mass graves, and the disposal of bodies by the Iraqis.

Drawings made by Kurdish refugee children in Turkey illustrate the chemical weapon attack.

There are continual reports of massacres of Kurdish civilians by the Iraqi army.

Many children in the refugee camps in Turkey are still suffering from burns and other medical problems. Doctors who examine the children say that these burns are the result of chemical weapons.

9 The United Nations

Lesson One

Aim

To explore peacemaking.

Objectives

To explore peacemaking in everyday life; to investigate the work of the UN; to examine the role of the UN in peacekeeping.

Resources

Information Sheet 49; Activity Sheet 50.

Method

1 Warm up activity. Use the situation on Activity Sheet 50 with the two members of the family to start discussion on peacekeeping and the difficulties it presents. Divide the class into groups to work out what responses might be made and then feed back into the larger group.

2 Read through the first sections of Information sheet 49, about the purpose of the UN and the nature of the Security Council.

3 Introduce the second activity on Activity Sheet 50, and ask the class to read through the peacekeeping section of the Information Sheet. They then fill in the answers in groups. Feed back to the class for a final debate on the role of a group such as the UN – should it, for example, be a world army that can invade countries to stop wars taking place?

'We the peoples of the United Nations determined to save succeeding generations from the scourge of war ...'
from Preamble to UN Charter

The Purposes of the United Nations

● To maintain international peace and **security**, and to that end: to take effective collective measures for the removal of threats to peace.

● To develop friendly relations among nations based on respect for human rights.

● To take other appropriate measures to strengthen universal peace.

● To achieve international co-operation in the solving of international problems.

● To be a centre for harmonising the actions of nations in the attainment of these common ends.

When the United Nations was set up in 1945 it was intended that the collective strength of UN members would be used to deter or punish aggression. National armies were to be reduced, and the UN **Security Council** was to deploy military units for joint action. These aims have never been realised, apparently due to the five permanent members of the Security Council failing to agree on the types, scale and control of forces and facilities to be placed at the disposal of the Council.

The Security Council

This is probably the most well known of the United Nations' Councils. The Security Council consists of five permanent members (Republic of China, France, Russia [formerly the Soviet Union], United Kingdom, United States of America), and ten others members elected by the General Assembly.

The Council has 'primary responsibility' for maintaining peace. The **General Assembly** has undertaken to accept and carry out the Security Council's decisions.

The five permanent members have the power of **veto** on decisions made by the Council. This means that even when the majority of members of the Council are in favour of a proposal, if one of the permanent members votes 'no' then that proposal is defeated. Until about 1970 this power of veto was used mainly by the Soviet Union, but it has increasingly been used by the three western permanent members, especially the United States, usually on Middle Eastern or Southern African issues.

Peacekeeping

The UN uses two methods: sending soldiers as armed policemen; or observers to report on breaches of the peace. Armed

UN soldiers have to try to stop fighting without fighting, and to shoot only in self-defence. These are examples of the UN's peacekeeping activities:

a) The Congo
Zaire was once the Congo. Belgium granted it independence in 1960, and rival factions struggled for control until 1964. The UN were involved as peacekeepers, with the close involvement of the Secretary General, Dag Hammarskjöld.

b) The Middle East
The UN helped Britain to run Palestine in 1948. The area was partitioned between Jews and Arabs, in an uneasy truce. A Swedish Count, in charge of the military observers, was killed in September 1948.

c) UNEF
The Suez crisis was settled in 1956 when Britain, France and Israel agreed to remove their troops from Egypt so long as the UN Emergency Force was stationed along the border with Israel. They stayed until 1967.

d) 1973 crisis
War broke out between Israel and Egypt again, and the UN forces were a buffer between these two sides, and between Israel and Syria.

e) Lebanon
The UN forces have been in Lebanon in 1978 and 1985 when civil war raged.

f) Bosnia
The UN presence in Bosnia in the 1990s has been controversial because they were forced to stand by while people were deported and sometimes massacred.

Social and Economic Work

a) **UNICEF (The UN International Children's Fund)**
This agency relies on voluntary donations, including funds from governments. Requests for help are made from a country, and the UNICEF board considers this 'without discrimination on the grounds of race, creed, nationality, status or political belief.' UNICEF has five objectives:

(i) improve health of children and mothers e.g. immunisation

(ii) improve nutrition

(iii) provide or improve education

(iv) provide social services for mothers

(v) train welfare staff.

b) **World Health Organisation**
This is the largest group in size and budget. It aims to:

(i) provide information

(ii) provide training

(iii) provide disaster relief

(iv) eliminate diseases (e.g. smallpox and malaria)

c) **UNESCO (UN Educational Scientific and Cultural Organisation)**
The major task of this agency has been to combat illiteracy. UNESCO has been the least efficient group, and has been very costly.

The United Nations

All in the Family

Make up a situation where two members of a family have an argument. One of the parents has to try to settle this, but the two people do not want to at first. What might the person do to keep the peace?

A World Army

What means can the UN legally use to keep the peace? Should the UN be a world army that can force countries to stop fighting? List the advantages and disadvantages in the two columns below.

Advantages

_____

_____

_____

_____

_____

Disadvantages

_____

_____

_____

_____

_____

D Religion

Religion and War

Lesson One

AIMS

To explore attitudes to religion and the causes of war. To draw out a positive kernel in religious teaching that might not always be adhered to.

RESOURCES

Activity Sheet 51, A3 paper, marker pens.

METHOD

1 Give out copies of Sheet 51. Divide the class into four or five groups. They work on the first question in their groups for a few minutes. Then feedback to the rest of the class.

2 Work on question two in their groups, and then feedback.

3 Debate 'Does religion cause wars?'. Explain that the wars they might have mentioned have deeper causes than religion, e.g. trouble in Bosnia, past conflict in Northern Ireland. They are about politics, who holds the power and who owns the land. Perhaps people will use any excuse to fight?

4 Work on the three speech balloons in groups. Feedback, and select the best ones. Have these groups draw them up neatly on A3 paper for display later.

5 Read through the section on the Golden Rule. Point out that this teaching is at the heart of the religions. Is it always lived out? In their groups, get them to rewrite the Golden Rule in contemporary, streetwise terms. Choose the best one as a class, and write this out on A3 paper to make a banner.

Lesson Two

AIM

To investigate attitudes to war as a moral duty in some religious traditions.

RESOURCES

Activity Sheets 52, 53; Information Sheets 54, 55, 56.

METHOD

1 Divide the class into five groups. Each group receives one of the sheets, so that each group looks at one different religion. Give them the question, 'Why do some religious people think it is their duty to fight in a war? Does this mean that they do not care about peace?' They read the material and prepare a presentation based upon this – spoken, acted, artistic, whatever they prefer. Give about 25 minutes for this.

2 Listen to the presentations in turn, allowing a couple of minutes for questions and feedback after each one.

3 Round off the lesson by pointing out that some people in religions have very strong feelings about war and do not think it is ever right to fight in one. There are different points of view.

Lesson Three

AIM

To explore the pacifist tradition in religions.

RESOURCES

Gandhi video; Activity Sheets 57–59; Information Sheet 55.

METHOD

1 Give out Activity Sheet 57. Introduce the character of Gandhi and the term ahimsa. Show the opening clip of *Gandhi*, where he is killed and the massive funeral. Then show him in action in South Africa, up to the meeting in the hall. Finally, show him in India, on the salt march.

2 Work through Activity Sheet 57, in class discussion.

3 Divide the class into three groups, and distribute Activity Sheets 58, 59 and Information Sheet 55. Their job is to present a brief talk on the pacifist teaching of each of these religions, and, if time, to engage in creative work.

The Buddhist group designs a peace pagoda to remember the innocents who have suffered in Bosnia.

The Jewish group draw a disarmament poster, showing modern weapons being turned into tools to save the environment.

The Christian group work out a role play about protest. They stage a demonstration and refuse to co-operate when threatened.

If desired, this lesson could be extended to a second. Perhaps the presentations and works of art could be videoed.

Lesson Four

AIM

To explore attitudes to just war and pacifist ideas in the film *The Mission*.

RESOURCES

The Mission video, Activity Sheet 60.

METHOD

1 Show all or part of the film depending upon how much time you want to give over to this. You will need three average lessons to show it all and do the follow up work. The film falls neatly into three sections:

(i) The establishment of the mission above the falls and Mendoza's murder of his brother.

(ii) Mendoza does penance and joins the mission. The brothers build up a wonderful community.

(iii) The Portuguese are about to take over the mission territories and want to enslave the tribes there. The Cardinal arrives to ajudicate. The verdict goes against the mission, and the final battle takes place.

Draw out the roles of Mendoza and Gabriel as typical proponents of the just war and the pacifist positions. Mendoza believes it is his duty to take up arms again and protect the innocent.

2 Discuss how Mendoza and Gabriel represent the two positions.

3 Discuss the question, 'What would you have done?' as on the sheet.

51 ACTIVITY SHEET
Does Religion Cause Wars?

1 List any wars that are being fought at the moment in the world.

2 Are any of these linked with religion? Do you know which religion?

3 Fill in the three speech balloons with ideas to answer the question, 'Does religion cause wars?'

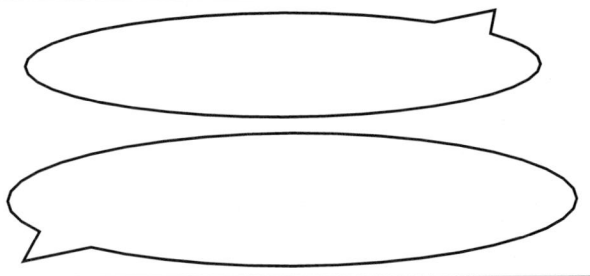

4 What do the religions teach?

'Love your neighbour as yourself.' (Christianity)

'One should seek for others the happiness one desires for oneself.' (Buddhism)

'Let none of you treat your brother in a way he himself would dislike to be treated.' (Islam)

Although religious differences can sometimes cause wars, the same basic moral teaching is at the heart of all religions: '**What you do to someone else is what you should expect to be done to you**.' This is known as 'the Golden Rule'. The founders of the faiths said things like 'Love your neighbour' and yet their words have been used to justify wars.

Perhaps religion can be used in a bad way or a good way, just as politics can cause wars or try to make peace. Then again, perhaps people think that sometimes it is necessary to fight a war to put something right (the 'just war' idea).

Hinduism – Dharma

One Hindu response to fighting in a war is to say it is your duty to fight in a just cause. **Dharma** is the Indian word for duty. This is taught in one of the most popular Hindu Scriptures, the Gita. The Gita begins before a large battle between rivals for the throne. Prince Arjuna is in his royal chariot and his charioteer is Krishna, who in Hindu belief was an appearance of Vishnu (God) on earth. Arjuna is troubled about the battle. He does not want to fight because his friends and family are on both sides. It is not worth winning the crown at the expense of killing them.

Krishna teaches that it is Arjuna's dharma to fight and encourages him that he cannot actually kill the souls (atman) of his friends and family. Only their bodies will die, but the souls will live on and be reborn.

'When a man knows him as never-born, everlasting, neverchanging, beyond all destruction, how can that man kill a man, or cause another to kill?

As a man leaves an old garment and puts on one that is new, the Spirit leaves his mortal body and then puts on one that is new.

Weapons cannot hurt the Spirit and fire can never burn him . . .'

(*Gita* 2:21–23)

'When I see my kinsmen, Krishna, who have come here on this field of battle,

Life goes from my limbs and they sink and my mouth is searing and dry; a trembling overcomes my body, and my hair shudders in horror . . . I cannot forsee any glory if I kill my own kinsmen in the sacrifice of battle . . .

Facing us in the field of battle are teachers, fathers and sons; grandsons, grandfathers, wives' brothers; mothers' brothers and fathers of wives . . .' (*Gita* 1:29–34)

Gita – Hindu holy book, 'The Song of God'
dharma – duty
atman – soul/spirit

1   How would you feel if you had to fight friends and family, but knew that the cause was just?
2   What advice did Krishna give to Arjuna? Do you think this was helpful?
3   What did Krishna teach about the soul?

> ITS MY MORAL DUTY TO DEFEND MY COUNTRY. I CANNOT JUST STAND BY AND SEE PEOPLE SUFFER

> JESUS WANTS US TO LIVE IN PEACE

Christians disagree about fighting in wars. Some Christians are pacifists, rejecting all war, and others follow the 'just war' theory. They believe it is moral to fight if it is for a just cause and it is the last resort.

Some Christians feel that some of the stories of Jesus suggest that it might be all right to use force for a good cause.

Jesus turned over the money changers' tables in the Temple.

Jesus Goes to the Temple

It was almost time for the Passover Festival, so Jesus went to Jerusalem. There in the Temple he found men selling cattle, sheep, and pigeons, and also the money-changers sitting at their tables. So he made a whip from cords and drove all the animals out of the Temple, both the sheep and the cattle; he overturned the tables of the money-changers and scattered their coins; and he ordered the men who sold the pigeons, "Take them out of here! Stop making my Father's house a market-place!" His disciples remembered that the scripture says, "My devotion to your house, O God, burns in me like a fire." (*John* 2:13–17)

Jesus healed a centurion's servant.

THIS MAN REALLY DESERVES YOUR HELP. HE LOVES OUR PEOPLE, AND HE BUILT A SYNAGOGUE FOR US

Jesus Heals a Roman Officer's Servant

When Jesus had finished saying all these things to the people, he went to Capernaum. A Roman officer there had a servant who was very dear to him; the man was sick and about to die. When the officer heard about Jesus, he sent some Jewish elders to ask him to come and heal his servant. They came to Jesus and begged him earnestly, "This man really deserves your help. He loves our people and he himself built a synagogue for us."

So Jesus went with them. He was not far from the house when the officer sent friends to tell him, "Sir, don't trouble yourself. I do not deserve to have you come into my house, neither do I consider myself worthy to come to you in person. Just give the order, and my servant will get well. I, too, am a man placed under the authority of superior officers, and I have soldiers under me. I order this one, 'Go!' and he goes; I order that one, 'Come!' and he comes; and I order my slave, 'Do this!' and he does it."

Jesus was surprised when he heard this; he turned round and said to the crowd following him, "I tell you, I have never found faith like this, not even in Israel!"

The messengers went back to the officer's house and found his servant well.
(*Luke* 7:1–10)

Why do you think these two stories help some Christians feel they are justified to fight in a war?

Many people would use violence to help someone in need. If they saw an elderly person being mugged, and they had a knife, then they might threaten the mugger to drive him or her away. Sikhs carry a knife, a kirpan, with very much the same thought in mind. It is to be used only in self-defence, and they must not be the first to draw it.

The kirpan is one of the Five Ks, the special items that every baptised Sikh is to carry with him or her. These items were introduced by the tenth Guru of the Sikhs, Guru Gobind Singh. He taught his people to defend themselves if attacked, and to protect the weak. They were warriors for justice. Gobind Singh once said,

> When all efforts to restore peace prove useless and now words avail,
> Lawful is the flash of steel, it is right to draw the sword.

Sikhs believe that the way of peace is better, and true peace is a gift from God:

> The Lord is the giver;
> The Lord is the haven of peace;
> The peace that reigns on snow-clad mountains.
> (*Granth*)

Guru – teacher
kirpan – sword
Granth – Sikh holy book

Others understand the old Scriptures as symbolic of our struggle against evil within ourselves, and that was the way primitive people understood this. They wiped out the enemy whose ways were different. Today we should tolerate and try to change people peacefully.

Some Jews are pacifists, pointing to the tradition of Shalom, peace, in the Scriptures:

> And they beat their swords into ploughshares and their spears into pruning hooks; nation shall not lift up sword against nation, neither shall they learn war any more.
> (*Isaiah* 2:4)

There are various traditions in Judaism. In general, Jews see war as a last resort, but accept it as their duty in self-defence. Much debate surrounds 'discretionary wars' where the nation takes action before they are attacked to stop an invasion or slaughter from occurring. This is seen to refer only to threats to the borders of Israel. The Rabbis follow ideas such as,

> No war may be waged against a nation that has not attacked Israel.

In the Hebrew Scriptures, though, some of the ancient Hebrews were commanded by God to fight wars, such as Joshua as he drove tribes out of the land of Canaan. Some rabbis believe that God can still command wars to be fought today, and it is a Jew's religious duty to take part.

Shalom, the Hebrew word for peace.

Rabbi – teacher
Shalom – peace

56 INFORMATION SHEET
Islam

Muslims believe that war is to be waged only in self-defence. The word 'Jihad' means struggle, a struggle against evil. The greater jihad is the struggle against evil in ourselves. The lesser jihad is a fight against an enemy in a war.
The name of the religion comes from an Arabic word, 'slm' which can mean 'peace'. The idea is that by submitting to the will of God, a person can find peace in their life.

From the Qur'an . . .

> Fight in the way of God with those who fight with you, but aggress not: God loves not the aggressors.
> (*Sura* 2:187)

Muslims should not attack first.

> If the enemy inclines towards peace, then you should also incline towards peace. (*Sura* 8:61)

Muslims are not to seek revenge. If peace is negotiated during a war, this should be welcomed, and they should show mercy.

> Let there be no compulsion in religion.
> (*Sura* 2:256)

Muslims must not force others to convert to their faith.

> And those who are slain in the way of God . . . He will admit them to Paradise . . . (*Sura* 47:7)

Hadith (the traditional sayings of the Prophet Muhammad) forbids Muslims to kill women, the elderly, children, and monks and nuns. The bodies of the enemy must not be mutilated.

> **Jihad** – struggle
> **Qur'an** – Muslim holy book
> **Hadith** – 'sayings of Muhammad'

Another response in Hinduism is **ahimsa**. This was taught by Mohandas Gandhi, who led India to independence from Britain in 1947. Ahimsa means 'non-violence'. You speak out, protest, march, demonstrate, disobey orders, all to make your point, but you never use violence. Non-violence is not passive, though. You do not just stand by and let things happen. As Gandhi said,

> The first principle of non-violent action is that of non-co-operation with everything humiliating . . . the masses have a weapon which enables a child, a woman, or even a decrepit old man to resist the mightiest government.

The scene above is from Tiananmen Square in China in 1988. Many peaceful demonstrators had been hurt or killed by the troops. One man held up a tank. His courage shamed the soldiers and made the news worldwide. If enough people acted like this, governments would have to back down. This is the principle behind ahimsa.

Gandhi developed his teachings from the Jain religion in India, which does not harm any living beings, even insects, and the teaching of Jesus in the Sermon on the Mount where he says that you should bless and pray for your enemies. Gandhi put ahimsa into practice in South Africa when he was a young lawyer. He led a demonstration against new laws that forced Asians to carry passbooks with them everywhere. This made them feel like second class citizens. Eventually, the government backed down, though Gandhi spent some time in prison. In India, in 1930, he led a march to the sea to make salt, in protest against a new law passed by the British which forbade home production of salt and placed a tax on salt that was sold.

> **ahimsa** – refusing to use violence
> **Jainism** – an Indian religion that respects all living things

> 1 Do you agree that ahimsa is a weapon that can force governments to change their minds?
> 2 List all the forms of non-violent protest that you can think of.
> 3 Can you think of any situations where it would be very hard to use ahimsa?

Buddhism

Buddhists are committed to non-violence and pacifism. Buddhists seek to develop inner peace and they follow the Noble Eightfold Path taught by the Buddha that leads to peace and enlightenment. The picture of a meditating Buddha below shows the peaceful quality that Buddhists want to find in their lives.

Some Buddhists build pagodas as monuments to peace, and sometimes make peace gardens, too. There is a peace pagoda in Battersea Park in London.

A Buddhist Scripture, the Dhammapada, says:

> Though one conquer a thousand times a thousand men in battle, he who conquers himself is the greatest warrior.
>
> Hatred does not cease by hatred; hatred ceases only by love. This is the eternal law.

Buddha – 'The Enlightened One'
Enlightenment – find a peaceful, just way of living
Dhammapada – a Buddhist scripture
pagoda – a building that represents peace

---

1 What desires do we have that are not easy to control? How might these harm ourselves and others?
2 Why do Buddhists think war will not solve anything?

One of the prophecies about the birth of the Messiah said,

> A child is born to us!
> A son is given to us!
> And he will be our ruler.
> He will be called, 'Wonderful Counsellor',
> 'Mighty God', 'Eternal Father', 'Prince of Peace'.
> (*Isaiah* 9:6)

Christians call Jesus the Prince of Peace. Some feel that to follow him, they have got to be pacifists, following non-violence. They point to several verses where Jesus seems to be a pacifist.

> 'Happy are those who work for peace; God will call them his children!' (*Matthew* 5:9)

> 'You have heard that it was said, "An eye for an eye, and a tooth for a tooth." But now I tell you: do not take revenge on someone who wrongs you. If anyone slaps you on the right cheek, let him slap you on the left cheek too.' (*Matthew* 5:38–39)

> Then they came up, arrested Jesus, and held him tight. One of those who was with Jesus drew his sword and struck at the High Priest's slave, cutting off his ear. Jesus said to him, 'All who take the sword will die by the sword.' (*Matthew* 26:50–51)

> Why do you think these verses make some Christians become pacifists?

The Mission is a film about the Jesuit missionaries in Latin America in the 1750s. The Jesuits were a group of monks who set up communities to help the native tribes and to teach them the Christian faith. The film is about Mendoza, a ruthless slave trader, who kills his brother in a duel, and is so filled with guilt, that he joins the Jesuits and works peacefully with the Guarani tribe whom he used to capture and kill. Father Gabriel leads the mission. The mission is on land which is about to be taken up by the Portuguese, who want to make slaves of the tribespeople. The monks must choose whether to go or stay. If they stay, do they fight with the Guarani against the Portuguese, or do they offer no resistance?

In the final scene, Mendoza finds his old weapons again and decides to fight for a just cause. Father Gabriel leads a service in the open air as the soldiers close in. He is killed, carrying blessed communion bread. Sadly, the tribespeople are slaughtered, and the rest of the monks are killed.

> This film highlights the dilemma faced by many Christians, 'Should I fight or not?' If you were one of the monks, what would you have done, and why?

E The Big If

① Conversion

Lesson One

AIM

To introduce the concept of arms conversion.

RESOURCES

Information Sheets 61, 62 (one copy per student).

METHOD

This activity will take 60 minutes; with option 4, another 30 minutes.

1 Give out the Information Sheets.

2 Ask students to compile a list of 'Dos and Don'ts' for companies embarking on arms conversion. For example:

Do
try and arrange joint ventures with other companies.

Don't
forget the quality of civilian goods need not be as high as for military goods.

3 Ask the students to discuss what they think about arms conversion.

4 Ask the students to write to some British arms firms (names given below) asking the company what they are doing about converting away from military production and why. Suggest they use the ideas from their 'Dos and Don'ts' list, using the information as concrete examples of successful conversion initiatives.

British Aerospace plc

General Electric Company

Lucas

Vickers Shipbuilding and Engineering Ltd (VSEL)

Rolls Royce plc

Vickers Defence Systems (unrelated to VSEL)

Lesson Two

AIM

To introduce the concept of conversion from military expenditure and technology to civilian needs.

RESOURCES

The Big If video, Activity Sheet 63.

METHOD

1 Introduce and explain the term 'conversion'. Read the story of collecting for a kidney machine on Activity Sheet 63 to put this into context.

2 Watch *The Big If* with follow up discussion.

3 Read through the rest of Activity Sheet 63 and work through the suggested activities.

Lesson Three

AIM

To enable students to think about alternative visions of the future.

RESOURCES

Activity Sheet 64.

METHOD

1 Visualisation exercise. Close your eyes and imagine how the world will be in the future. Collect those ideas and discuss.

2 Discuss what can be done to change things for the future (e.g. the Body Shop trying to work with ethical principles).

3 Read through Activity Sheet 64 and work on the activities.

61 INFORMATION SHEET
Possibilities for Arms Conversion

'Arms conversion' is a process whereby a company stops making military goods and starts making civilian goods instead. Well known phrases such as 'Swords into Ploughshares' and 'Tanks into Tractors' refer to this process.

During the Cold War (see below), arms manufacturers across east and west Europe and North America faced a steady demand from their governments who were all eager to be militarily superior to their adversaries. This desire not to fall behind in the arms race meant big profits for arms companies. While most of their weapons were sold to their own government and allies, arms exports to Southern countries became an additional way to make money.

When the Cold War ended in the late 1980s, arms companies faced a massive decline in orders. Not only were home governments less interested in buying large amounts of expensive high-tech weaponry, governments across the South simply could no longer afford to buy. Faced with this sudden loss of a previously very secure and highly profitable market, arms companies have had to make drastic changes.

Some of them have tried to increase their arms exports but this market is becoming increasingly competitive as arms firms across the industrialised world try to find a buyer. Other companies are sacking thousands of employees, in an attempt to stay profitable. Others have decided that the best strategy is simply to 'convert' – stop making products for the military and start making and selling products for the public instead – goods like passenger aircraft rather than fighter jets, railway carriages rather than battleships, more modern electronics and communications goods for personal use such as video phones and satellite dishes. Some have even put their expertise into making equipment for people with disabilities.

Moving into the consumer market is a difficult step for these companies but many people say it is a vital step if these companies are going to survive. The newspaper cutting on the next page focuses on how some of the big arms companies in the United States are attempting 'conversion', looks into the difficulties they are facing, and shows how some of them are overcoming these difficulties.

> **'Cold War'** refers to the conflict of ideologies between the former communist Soviet Union and the capitalist United States, and their respective political allies. Known as the two Superpowers, these two countries' opposing political viewpoints, and the accompanying nuclear and conventional arms race, overshadowed the political and economic shape of the world from the end of World War II until the late 1980s. 'Cold' refers to the fact that the conflict never became an actual 'shooting' or 'hot' war between the Superpowers.

Fighting on Foreign Soil

US defence contractors find they have to work hard to compete in the civilian market, says Victoria Griffith

Fighting on foreign soil

In a bid to ease the US defence industry's suffering over more military spending cuts, President Bill Clinton has been zealously promoting the concept of "dual use" – the civilian and commercial use of technologies originally developed for the Pentagon.

The administration has even pledged US$500m (£330m) to help former defence contractors convert their plants to non-military production. Yet many groups in the industry are discovering that although the potential rewards are enticing, the task of switching technologies from the military to the civilian and commercial sectors is daunting.

One of the biggest hurdles facing military manufacturers is their lack of a strong marketing capability. Many defence groups have no advertising department, no distribution network and a limited sales force, making it difficult for them to sell their products to a large market.

"Most defence groups haven't got the slightest idea how to sell a product on the mass market," says Greg Frisby, president of Frisby Airborne,

a Long Island-based hydraulics group and defence contractor. "That's not surprising. After all, they spend most of their time dealing with a single customer, the Pentagon."

Marketing is not the only problem the industry faces. Civilian and commercial work can also present cash-flow difficulties, as companies used to getting paid in military-style instalments for continuing work are forced to wait until after delivery to receive any payment.

Defence contractors are also snowed under by the astronomical wages they are forced to pay their highly educated workforce. "We pay mechanics $18 an hour because we need their level of skills to produce military-standard products," says Robert O'Brien, public affairs director at McDonnell Douglas. "But a lot of consumer products don't need that level of expertise, and we can't compete with someone who's paying employees $6 an hour to put out the same product."

The industry also complains about the Pentagon's stringent specifications, which are

so demanding that they price the product out of the consumer market. "There are 15 pages of specifications for ketchup in the military, and you can extrapolate from that," says Smith.

"Obviously, your average consumer is not willing to pay the extra cost it takes to meet those specifications. The consumer is performance-oriented, the military specifications-oriented. They are completely different markets," he adds.

Despite the myriad difficulties involved with conversion, defence contractors say that in the face of a diminished federal military budget, it is essential to find new markets. Companies insist that non-military applications can be found for most of their products, and they have come up with a number of successes.

"There's clearly not much of a market outside the military for B-52 bombers or nuclear missiles but most products can be adapted in some way," says Noel Longuemare, head of the systems development and technology division at Westinghouse Electric Corporation in Baltimore.

Westinghouse's defence arm, Westinghouse Electronic Systems, has been hailed by Clinton as a conversion success story. The group reduced its reliance on defence work from 84 per cent in 1986 to 73 per cent today. Westinghouse accomplished this by successfully marketing its military surveillance technology as air traffic control equipment, and selling military security products to civilian police forces.

By marketing thermal control systems to the oil industry, Frisby Airborne has made an even bigger switch, from being 95 per cent defence-dependent in 1985 to just 25 per cent today. Boeing, the aircraft manufacturer, has long maintained a balance between military and commercial sales, and McDonnell Douglas has successfully adapted a number of military aeroplane technologies to the commercial market.

Most of the success stories, though, have taken place outside the mass market. "Selling to non-defence sectors of the government is a good option for defence groups wanting to make a switch,'' says Smith. "One of the things defence companies know how to deal with is red tape and bureaucracy. Dealing with the civilian side of the government is far closer to the sort of business we're used to than consumer products.''

Another option for defence groups is to sell big-ticket items in low-volume markets. Both McDonnell Douglas and Boeing have been successful at marketing their aircraft to the commercial as well as the military sector.

Still, some defence contractors insist that the mass market is an option if it is approached in the right way. Westinghouse, for instance, has joined Chrysler in a joint venture to develop technology for electric cars. "Joint ventures are a good way to go because you can join with companies who know the markets well,'' Longuemare says.

Although conversion may be the wave of the future, defence groups are quick to point out that there is still a lot of money to be made in sales to the Pentagon. "I think the main point is that the communication between the commercial and defence sides must be improved,'' says Russ Young, a spokesman for Boeing. "In many cases the same technology can be used in both areas."

Still, companies are learning from their mistakes and are gradually finding niche markets in which they can compete effectively. "Dual use" may not be the answer to all their problems but most contractors are ready to give conversion a try. With the once deep pockets of the Pentagon becoming ever more shallow, most feel they have no other choice.
Financial Times 22.6.93

(63) ACTIVITY SHEET
Disarmament and Conversion

Case Study: The Lucas Aerospace Plan

'The government, that is me the taxpayer, buys Harrier jump jets and medical equipment like kidney machines. Lucas says it's profitable to produce Harriers but not profitable to produce kidney machines. People are dying because there aren't enough kidney machines to go round. We collected pennies on street corners and in pubs to buy a kidney machine for a little boy who was dying because the National Health Service couldn't provide one. The money was raised in no time. I wonder if somehow things were reversed and it became profitable to produce kidney machines and unprofitable to produce aircraft, how many people would give pennies to government ministers or civil servants on street corners when they wanted a new Harrier or Tornado?'
Lucas Aerospace Worker

In 1975, as now, there were many cuts being made in military expenditure. At the time defence contracts accounted for 50% of Lucas Aerospace's work. To avoid massive cuts in jobs if the arms contracts were lost, the Lucas Aerospace Combined Shop Stewards Committee worked out a strategy for conversion. The Committee represented all 14,000 workers in all of the 17 British sites of Lucas Aerospace.

The process to set up the plan involved consultation with all grades of workers, and eventually twelve products were selected. The projects chosen were selected to achieve balance between long- and short-term projects; projects of direct use to the UK and for newly emergent countries; projects which required high initial investment and those which could be started right away.

Products selected included telecheiric machines (electro-mechanical extensions to the human body and remotely controlled by the operator, for use in dangerous environments), alternative energy sources (wind generators, solar collectors, turbines for tidal power stations) and medical equipment (portable life-support systems for ambulances, kidney machines, aids for the disabled, sight substituting aids for the blind).

The Lucas Proposal was believed to have been capable of producing enough work for all Lucas Aerospace employees, and for thousands of others.

---

1 You are on the board of an armaments factory. You wish to convert production to civilian use.
   a) Make a list of products you believe are marketable. (You may wish to brainstorm ideas in groups.)
   b) In pairs or small groups devise an advertising campaign for your new product.
   c) You may want a slogan, a poster, radio or television advertisement. Make it clear you are converting from military manufacturing, and say why you are doing this.

A Vision for the Future

Whoops!
Too late to learn now.

'You can never plan the future by the past'

Edmund Burke

The Visitor from outer space was allowed time to become acclimatised to the Earth's atmosphere, and was then shown some aspects of our civilisation. On the third day of the tour, the visitor was invited to the Ministry of Defence. The top brass at the Ministry were naturally keen to hear how the visitor's planet equipped its armed forces. The visitor told them: 'I think we can pride ourselves that on our planet, no expense is spared to provide our services with the most up-to-date equipment.'

'What sort of guns do you use?' asked one of the generals.

'Guns? Why should we need guns?' The visitor looked puzzled.

'Why, to deal with your enemies.'

'Oh yes, our enemies: earthquakes, floods, hurricanes and so on. Of course this is where our army is most useful – a trained group of people ready to rush to any area where there is a disaster, provide medical treatment and food, and help to rebuild shattered homes and communications. But I'm still not sure what you mean about guns.'

Another general said: 'What we really wanted to know was, how are your services armed?'

The visitor replied: 'Our services are armed with all the necessary equipment that any army needs – ambulances, field hospitals, mobile kitchens, and all kinds of agricultural machinery to help restore the lands after floods and typhoons. Our Cavalry, of course, is specially trained in the use of horses for ploughing; our Pioneer Corps is expert at digging ditches and sewers; while our Parachute Regiment can be flown to a disaster area anywhere on the planet within a few hours.'

'We are very interested in hearing about your disaster work,' said another general. 'Our own forces occasionally do the same thing. But this must be only a small part of your army's work. Can't you tell us more about how they are usually employed?'

'Certainly," replied the visitor. 'It is true, thank goodness, that there are not so many disasters as to keep our army permanently occupied, and they have plenty of other duties to keep them busy. For example, the Cavalry normally does ploughing and other agricultural jobs at home, and they are often engaged abroad in helping less fortunate countries with their agriculture. Similarly, our Catering Corps, besides providing the best food for hungry people anywhere on our planet, is kept pretty busy at home with its 'Meals on Wheels' scheme that delivers regular meals to old people and invalids who can't cook for themselves but want to remain fairly independent. The Signals Corps likewise help old people by fixing up free telephones and radios for them.

By this time some of the military men were becoming restless. One of them, with ill-concealed impatience snapped: 'This is all very fine, but you still haven't said anything of preparations for conflict.'

'I beg your pardon,' said the visitor. 'You must forgive me for overlooking that very important part of the army's work – preparations for conflict.' The generals looked happier.

'We recognise,' the visitor continued, 'that there is bound to be conflict between people so long as they are different from one another, and that such conflict – while sometimes healthy – can be extremely dangerous. So our Intelligence Corps is given the important task of foreseeing and investigating conflicts. They watch out for areas where injustice or discontent may arise, and try to forestall such dangerous things as inequality of opportunities or the denial of full expression to a minority group. In this way, we can foresee potential conflicts and try to put right any injustice or disagreement before it leads to hostility. Reconciliation is usually possible, as long as potential conflict is dealt with before bitterness arises.'

The generals were impatient again. One of them said curtly, 'You still haven't said anything about war!'

'What is war?' asked the visitor.

I   Write a short piece about how you think the world might be in 100 years time. You may find it useful to consider what things were like a hundred years ago, and how things have changed in that amount of time.
or
There are many fantasy and science fiction books around. Do you think the view of the future presented in one of them you have read recently is probable or possible? Discuss.

2   'Militarily we are highly advanced, but morally we still live in the stone age.' (Bruce Kent, *Building the Global Village*.) What do you think Bruce Kent means? Do you agree?

3   (Optional) You may like to write a manifesto for peace, or express your hopes for the future through a drawing, painting, piece of poetry, sculpture or collage either in groups or on your own.

Think about the good things going on in the world now, e.g. all the people who are campaigning to save the rainforests.

If these good things were developed and enlarged, what might the world be like?

F Appendix

Alternatives to Despair – What is Peace Education?

I was asked to address this question in February of this year, when asked to speak at conference on the theme of 'Children and War' in Osijek, in northern Croatia. Osijek was still wearing the scars of shelling, still mourning the death of hundreds of men, women and children, coping with the trauma of broken lives, of thousands of refugees and displaced people. What could teachers, social workers and psychologists do in a climate of grief mingled with hatred? What role could peace education play? My answer was that peace education is a *process of seeking alternatives to despair*.

I see that process of seeking alternatives to despair as a basic educational priority not just in the Balkans. It is just as essential in Hungary, from where I returned a few days ago after working with teachers, teacher trainers and psychologists, and it is just as essential in Britain.

The first thing to emphasise is that Peace Education is a PROCESS, it is not a set of easy answers to the world's problems.

It is a process which starts with ourselves as individuals and the young people in our care. So its first priority is to build an AFFIRMING climate. This means helping young people to form a positive self-image, which is not dependent on academic or sporting achievement, or the school's position in league tables, nor is it dependent on being male or female or being of a particular religion, ethnic group or nationality. It means valuing ourselves for what we are and valuing others for what they are. Unfortunately schools often succeed in enhancing in pupils either a negative image of themselves, or of others or both. Some

pupils react by absenting themselves (as the recent truancy figures indicate), some by quiet withdrawal, some by asserting themselves at the expense of others by becoming bullies, some by exhibiting disruptive behaviour and often getting excluded from school. It should be noted that one of the things Hitler, Mussolini and Stalin had in common was that they had all been expelled from educational institutions.

The second ingredient of the process is to build a LISTENING climate. This means taking time to practice the skills of non-judgemental listening, which enables people to hear what the other person is really saying, whether we happen to agree or not and encourages people to express their feelings, needs and interest, as well as their opinions without fear. Sadly, for all the words that are spoken in schools, there are many schools where little real communication takes place.

The third ingredient of the process is to build a CO-OPERATIVE climate. This means helping young people to learn to work together, play together and to build trust. While some competition, which encourages individuals to do their best, can be healthy, an atmosphere which continually produces winners and losers is damaging. Learning to co-operate with others is a basic priority.

I said that Peace Education is a process, a process of seeking alternatives to despair. The *seeking* and *alternatives* needs emphasis, because peace education is both experiential and experimental. Hence it's fourth ingredient is PROBLEM-SOLVING. This means helping young people to regard the problems and conflicts of life at all levels from the personal to the international as potential growing points. To learn to analyse and state problems in non-judgemental terms, to learn to recognise other people's needs and fears and to express their own, to learn to attack the problem and not the other people involved with the problem and to look for options for action other than 'fight or flight'. It does not mean 'passivism', that is the passive acceptance of injustice. It means generating creative ideas, alternatives for action. Above all, it means looking for alternatives to violence in every situation of conflict. It also means a climate where solutions to problems are not dictated by those in authority, but the responsibility for problem-solving is shared.

The fifth ingredient is to build a HUMAN RIGHTS climate. This means more than teaching about human rights. It means creating an atmosphere where young people become sensitive to the basic principles of universal civil, social and political rights and the shared responsibility for making those rights a reality. It means that schools and colleges must foster an ethos which reflects a framework of values based on the UN Universal Declaration and The European Convention on Human Rights. This should not be sterile knowledge, but a benchmark, a measure of our values by which the justice of proposed solutions to problems (whether within the classroom or in the national or international sphere) should be judged. It should lead to an appreciation of a limit to 'my rights' where they trample on other's, a sense of responsibility for each other's rights and skills for handling situations which arise when 'rights' come into conflict.

When working with teenagers, I often ask them if they think the world they will hand on to their grandchildren will be better or worse than the one they have inherited. In most groups there is a consensus of pessimism. This changed briefly in 1989/90 as the dramatic changes in central and eastern Europe brought the Cold War to an end and made the old symbols of despair, the escalating numbers of nuclear missiles, the iron curtain and the Berlin Wall, part of history. There was then a moment of hope that the 'new world order' would create an atmosphere of co-operation between east and west and between north and south which would enable humankind not only to turn back from the nuclear abyss, but to tackle the linked problems of threatening environmental disaster, poverty and famine arising out of unjust systems trade and debt and dependency.

One of the successes of both the formal education system and the media is that young people today are more aware of the threats to their future than at any time before. The danger is that they are left feeling powerless to do anything about it. Peace Education should, above all, be a process of empowerment. Not by giving superficial, easy answers, but by providing the basic skills for each individual to engage in non-violent creative problem-solving.

It is fashionable to talk about going 'back to basics'. What can be more basic than giving *hope* for the future? What is the use of league tables and SATs when so many of our young people despair of a future? Peace Education should serve to enable young people today to face the future with a sense of hope rather than despair. Hope is often associated with the unrealistic vision of no problems, of people living 'happily ever after' in effortless harmony and increasing prosperity. As that hope is continually unfulfilled, people turn again to despair which leads to distrust and violence. Real hope, therefore must be built on learning to face problems creatively and this is what Peace Education is about.

Tom Leimdorfer 20/11/93

The Seville Statement in Plain Words

The Seville Statement on Violence was written in 1986 by an international team of specialists for the United Nations. One of the main elements of the Statement says that war is a social invention, and that peace can be invented to replace it. In 1989 the Statement was adopted by UNESCO for use in programmes of education for peace and international understanding.

Introduction

This Statement is a message of hope. It says that peace is possible and that wars can be ended. It says that the suffering of war can be ended, the suffering of people who are injured and die, and the suffering of children who are left without home or family. It says that instead of preparing for war, we can use the money for things like teachers, books, and schools, and for doctors, medicines, and hospitals.

We who wrote this Statement are scientists from many countries, North and South, East and West. The Statement has been endorsed and published by many organizations of scientists around the world, including anthropologists, ethologists (animal behavior), physiologists, political scientists, psychiatrists, psychologists, and sociologists.

We have studied the problem of war and violence with today's scientific methods. Of course, knowledge is never final, and someday people will know better than we know today. But we have a responsibility to speak out on the basis of the latest information.

Some people say that violence and war cannot be ended because they are part of our natural biology. We say that is not true. People used to say that slavery and domination by race and sex were part of our biology. Some people even claimed they could prove these things scientifically. We now know they were wrong. Slavery has been ended and now the world is working to end domination by race and sex.

Five Propositions

1 It is scientifically incorrect when people say that war cannot be ended because animals make war and because people are like animals. First, it is not true because animals do not make war. Second, it is not true because we are not just like animals. Unlike animals, we have human culture that we can change. A culture that has war in one century may change and live at peace with their neighbors in another century.

2 It is scientifically incorrect when people say that war cannot be ended because it is part of human nature. Arguments about human nature cannot prove anything because our human culture gives us the ability to shape and change our nature from one generation to another. It is true that the genes that are transmitted in egg and sperm from parents to children influence the way we act. But it is also true that we are influenced by the culture in which we grow up and that we can take responsibility for our own actions.

3 It is scientifically incorrect when people say that violence cannot be

ended because people and animals who are violent are able to live better and have more children than others. Actually, the evidence shows that people and animals do best when they learn how to work well with each other.

4 It is scientifically incorrect when people say that we have to be violent because of our brain. The brain is part of our body like our legs and hands. They can all be used for cooperation just as well as they can be used for violence. Since the brain is the physical basis of our intelligence, it enables us to think of what we want to do and what we ought to do. And since the brain has a great capacity for learning, it is possible for us to invent new ways of doing things.

5 It is scientifically incorrect when people say that war is caused by 'instinct'. Most scientists do not use the term 'instinct' anymore because none of our behavior is so determined that it cannot be changed by learning. Of course, we have emotions and motivations like fear, anger, sex, and hunger, but we are each responsible for the way we express them. In modern war, the decisions and actions of generals and soldiers are not usually emotional. Instead, they are doing their jobs the way they have been trained. When soldiers are trained for war and when people are trained to support a war, they are taught to hate and fear an enemy. The most important question is why they are trained and prepared that way in the first place by political leaders and the mass media.

Conclusion

We conclude that we are not condemned to war and violence because of our biology. Instead, it is possible for us to end war and the suffering it causes. We cannot do it by working alone, but only by working together. However, it makes a big difference whether or not each one of us believes that we can do it. Otherwise, we may not even try. War was invented in ancient times, and in the same way we can invent peace in our time. It is up to each of us to do our part.

Recent Statements from the Catholic Church on Nuclear Weapons

Nuclear deterrence prevents genuine nuclear disarmament. It maintains an unacceptable hegemony over non-nuclear development for the poorest half of the world's population. It is a fundamental obstacle to achieving a new age of global security.

Archbishop Renato Martino
UN General Assembly, 1993

The Holy See considers nuclear disarmament to be one of the elements of general and complete disarmament. Nuclear disarmament – like nuclear non-proliferation – is an essential prerequisite for the elimination of the risk of nuclear war. It must however be accompanied by the abolition of all weapons of mass destruction and the limitation of conventional weapons. Nuclear States must be mindful of their specific responsibility to proceed with nuclear disarmament.

Vatican Delegation to the Nuclear Non-Proliferation Treaty Conference, 1995

I express my deep appreciation and strong support to all modern peacemakers. I do so especially by reason of the haunting memory of the atomic explosions which struck first Hiroshima and then Nagasaki in August 1945. They bear witness to the overwhelming horror and suffering caused by war: the final toll of that tragedy has not yet been entirely determined, nor has its cost in human terms yet been calculated, particularly when we consider what effect nuclear war has had and could still have on our thinking, our attitudes and our civilization. "To remember the past is to commit oneself to the future. To remember Hiroshima is to abhor nuclear war. To remember Hiroshima is to commit oneself to peace".

Pope John Paul II on the fiftieth anniversary of the end of World War II, May 1995

Militarism and the Environment

Facts

1 By 1989 approximately 550 nuclear reactors (more than the number in civil use on land) were on the world's warships and submarines. 50 nuclear warheads and 8 reactors now lie on the sea beds of the oceans as a result of accidents.

2 The Pentagon is the largest consumer of oil in the United States. The 200 billion barrels of oil it used in 1989 could run the US public transport system for 22 years.

3 One quarter of the world's jet fuel is used by military aircraft.

4 The military consumption of aluminium, copper, nickel and platinum, exceeds that of the entire Third World.

5 The world's armed forces are responsible for more than two-thirds of the ozone-depleting CFC113 released into the atmosphere.

6 The Pentagon generates five times more toxic waste than that produced by all the five major US chemical companies.

7 Nine million children die each year from preventable diseases. The cost of preventing such deaths is $2.5 billion: about two days of world military expenditure.

8 In the Vietnam War forests were defoliated by 50 million litres of Agent Orange. Between 1945 and 1982 Vietnam lost more than 80% of its original forest cover. To date only 1% of that cover has been successfully replaced.

9 Ground water in some aquifers at the Nevada Test Site is contaminated by tritium 3000 times in excess of safe drinking water standards. Plutonium contaminants have also been traced in the water and will be radioactive for 20,000 years, capable of causing cancer if ingested.

10 According to the US Department of Energy itself over half of all Nevada Underground Tests have leaked radiation into the atmosphere.

Statements on Militarism and the Environment

- Among the dangers facing the environment, the possibility of nuclear war, or military conflict of a lesser scale involving weapons of mass destruction is undoubtedly the greatest.

- The likely consequences of nuclear war make other threats to the environment pale into insignificance. Nuclear weapons represent a qualitatively new step in the development of warfare. One thermo-nuclear bomb can have an explosive power greater than that of all the explosives used in wars since the invention of gunpowder.

- The distorting effects of the 'arms culture' are most striking in the deployment of scientific personnel. Half a million scientists are employed on weapons research worldwide and they account for around half of all research and development expenditure.

- Global water use doubled between 1940 and 1980 and it is expected to double again by 2000 with two-thirds of the projected water use going to agriculture. Yet 80 countries with 40% of the world's population already suffer serious water shortage. There will be growing competition for water for irrigation, industry and domestic use.

(*The Brundtland Report 1987*, Our Common Future, Chapter 11: 'Peace, Security, Development and the Environment')

'Disarmament and other security issues are not on the [Rio 92] agenda but global discussions and international agreements [on environmental and development matters] are worthless without progress on these issues.'

(*M. Mostafa Tolbe, Director: United Nations Environmental Programme, January 1992*)

Imperial War Museum Education Service

In 1917 the government decided that a National War Museum should be set up to collect and display material relating to the Great War, which was still being fought. It was considered vitally important that the public and future generations should be aware of the various contributions and sacrifices that both men and women had made in Britain and the colonies, which led to the museum being given the title of Imperial War Museum. The Museum was formally established by Act of Parliament in 1920 and initially housed in the Crystal Palace and from 1924 to 1935, under very difficult conditions, it had its home at the Imperial Institute, South Kensington. In 1936 the Museum was reopened in its present home at Lambeth, in the building which used to be Bethlem Royal Hospital. At the outset of the Second World War, in 1939, the Museum's terms of reference were enlarged to cover both world wars and were later extended to include all military operations in which Britain and the Commonwealth have been involved since 1914. As the Museum goes through various stages of redevelopment, new areas of the collection can be shown to the public, and with the completion of additional galleries in 1996, the public can now see more of the post-1945 collection and information about recent conflicts.

The education department has an important role in communicating and interpreting the difficult subject area of war and conflict in this century to a wide age range of young people from 8–18 years. The education service was started about 25 years ago and has been developing ever since, constantly adapting to the ever changing needs of teachers and students. Younger children are introduced to the concepts of war and conflict in the 20th century, while older pupils are encouraged to develop their understanding of the causes and effects of conflict so that they can use their knowledge of the past to interpret present events. The Museum's collection provides a wide range of primary sources: artefacts, documents, photographs, paintings, oral history and film, which provide a unique opportunity to stimulate students' interest and further their ability to use evidence critically.

A wide range of teaching activities is also available, which are adapted to the requirements of the National Curriculum, mainly for history Key Stages 2 and 3 and GCSE, although other subjects across the curriculum can be catered for too. There are also special activities for sixth form students including conferences, lectures and study days, usually on a major historical theme but sometimes geared more towards English students doing war poetry or art students studying war art. For primary school children there are special teaching sessions available on life in the Second World War using artefacts, photographs and documents which bring alive the conditions and problems of wartime Britain.

For GCSE and KS3 pupils there is a wide range of study sessions: Britain and the Great War (KS3 only), Trench Warfare, Women in the First World War, The Home Front 1914–18 (including work on conscientious objectors), The Home Front 1939–45 and Nazi Germany 1933–39. In these sessions students have a unique opportunity to study and handle artefacts, documents, photographs, listen to oral history and watch original film.

Practical workshops are also arranged from wartime cooking to drama where students confront the issues and dilemmas which ordinary people had to face in a wartime situation. There are also practical art sessions connected to special exhibitions at the Museum.

A popular activity with school groups is the Blitz Experience, where an actor-interpreter in the role of an air raid warden takes children back in time to the Second World War and to the days of the Blitz. The Trench Experience is similar but this time the actor-interpreter, in the role of either a First World War soldier or a nurse in a Casualty Clearing Station, helps pupils to find out about life in the trenches during the First World War.

The education department is also involved in producing resources that can be used both in the Museum and back at school. An educational visits pack is available which contains a Museum handbook, master copies of a wide range of worksheets and information on how to get the most out of a visit. Facsimile document packs, audio-tapes, videos, posters, postcards and a variety of books are also available.

Nearly 80,000 students visit the Museum each year and about 80% of these receive some kind of education service (teaching session, Blitz or Trench Experience, film etc.). The number of schools (a maximum of twelve) and the size of groups (60 maximum) that can be accommodated on any one day are determined by the constraints of the building and its facilities. School groups can book a visit to the Museum free of charge through the education booking service providing they give at least 2 weeks notice. Demands on the service are ever increasing so it is a good idea to book early. If you would like to know more about the education service please ring: 0171 416 5313.

Useful Addresses

Peace Pledge Union
41b Brecknock Road
London N7 0BT
tel 0171 424 9444

Pax Christi
International Catholic Movement
for Peace
9 Henry Road
London N4 2LH
tel 0181 800 4612

Quaker Peace and Service
Friends House
Euston Road
London NW1 2BJ
tel 0171 387 3601

National Peace Council
88 Islington High Street
London N1 8EG
tel 0171 354 5200

Campaign for Nuclear Disarmament
162 Holloway Road
London N7 8DQ
tel 0171 700 2393

Imperial War Museum
Lambeth Road
London SE1 6HZ
tel 0171 416 5000
Education Service 0171 416 5313

Campaign Against Arms Trade
11 Goodwin Street
London N4 3HQ
tel 0171 281 0297

Oxford Development Education Centre
East Oxford Community Centre
Princes Street
Oxford OX4 1DD
tel 01865 790490

Development Education Association
29–31 Cowper Street
London EC2A 4AP
tel 0171 490 8108

Scientists for Global Responsibility
3 Down House
The Business Village
Broomhill Road
London SW18 4JQ
tel 0181 871 5175